# COWBOY GUITARS

It's a big roundup of those wonderful cowboy guitars
starting with the Gene Autry Model of 1932 through present day.

## By Steve Evans and Ron Middlebrook

## Forward by Roy Rogers, Jr.

Front cover photo –Steve Evans
1940 "Buck Jones" guitar made by Regal,
and sold through Montgomery Ward

Back cover photo – Steve Evans
Guitars from left
Early 1940s "Jerry the Yodeling Cowboy",
Mid 1950s "Roy Rogers"
Early 1940s "Red Foley"
1935 "Gene Autry",
Early 1940s "Corral Scene"

Color section layout: Shawn Brown
Layout: Matt Levonian, Melodie Jones, and Ron Middlebrook
Production: Ron Middlebrook

ISBN 1-57424-102-8
SAN 683-8022

Copyright © 2002 CENTERSTREAM Publishing
P.O. Box 17878 - Anaheim Hills, CA 92807

OCM 50555482

# Special Thanks

## to the many people that helped with this book.

There are several people to thank for helping with this book. They are Larry Briggs, Sylvain Acher, Brian Fischer, Eric Lenius, Steve and Paula Soest, Vicki Cwiok and Sears, Roebuck & Company, Amanda Crockett and Spiegel, Clare A. Dale, T. Eaton Company, Edouard D. Richard, Emmett Chism and Montgomery Ward, Maria Maccaferri, Calistus Alles, Rob Hood and Sears Canada, Helene Frost and Mattel Toys, Jim Gilcher and the Ohio Art Company, George Jefferson of Jefferson Manufacturing, John Elling, Dale Cameron, Chris Broadwell, Rob Friedman, Walter Carter, George Gruhn, Leonard Coulson, James Burkett, Tom Wheeler, Mike Longworth, DeWitt Nixon, Mike Newton, Jeff Dulfer, John Gima, Joe Schenkman, Fred Popovich, Larry Goldstein, UALR Library, Valerie Thwing and the Little Rock Library, Louise Lovett, Freeman Thomas, Albert Frazier, J.D. Hall, Barry Haver, Grant MacNeill, DeWitt Nixon, Chris Houston, Alex Vargy, Larry Dye, Guelph Civic Museum, Guelph Public Library, David Grahame, Pat O'Donnell, Len Farrell, Nick Clarke, Doug Fritts, Gil Hembree, Billy Herrell, Bob Boyd, Bob Fischer, Michael Stevens, Scott Waterhouse, Guy Logsdon, Don Castle, Audie Grider, John McGinty, Gloria & Les Evans, and several more helpful people.

# Photo Credits

## (contributor/photographer and page number)

Sylvain Acher #25, #27, #36, #74, #76, #81, #84, #94, #110, #158, #174, #175, #185 & #193; Sylvain Acher/Adam Henry of Mark Alexander Photography #36, #42 & #C12; Larry Briggs/Steve Evans #54, #60, #102, #C4, #C5, #C6, #116, #120, #123, #127, #149, #150, #151, #157, #167 & #178; James Burkett/Eliot Burkett #27, #33 & #121; Dale Cameron/Patrick Vrouwe #95, #118, #124, #150, #151 & #154; Mike Cherry #132; Leonard Coulson #40, #113 & #119; Bill Dye/Larry Dye #98; Archives of Ontario and T. Eaton Company #45, #59, #91 & #153; John Elling #120 & #147; Melissa Etheridge/Steve Evans #75 & #C13; Len Farrell #127; Brian Fischer #28, #37, #62, #97, #114, #121, #129, #132, #135, #164, #165, #172, #182, #183, #184, #185, #190, #191, #192 & #197; Brian Fischer/Thom Hindle #64; Rob Friedman/Randy Cole #125 & #165; Rob Friedman/Jennifer Sinclair #60; John Hargiss #172 & #184; Barry Haver #161; Eric Lenius/Matthew Sinn #34, #57, #66, #87 & #164; Elliot Mechanic #92; Rod Norwood/Steve Evans #179; Sears Canada #125; Sears, Roebuck Co. #20, #30, #82 & #134; Jesse Soest/Steve Soest #67; Michael Stevens #119 & #144; Bob Tanner #3 & #226; Stuart Williamson/Steve Evans #16. Several photos were also supplied by Steve Evans and Ron Middlebrook.

Steve Evans was nine years old when he became a guitar enthusiast. That is when he got his first guitar, a Harmony Stella. At eighteen years old he opened Jacksonville Guitar Center and at about the same time began collecting vintage guitars. Photographs of Steve's guitars have been published in several magazines and books. He has written many articles on cowboy guitars and is recognized as the leading authority on the subject.

He has assembled one of the largest collections of cowboy guitars in the world and this collection is on display as a small guitar museum at Jacksonville Guitar Center in Jacksonville, Arkansas.

He is married to wife Pam, and they have a lovely family with children Sarah, Jenna and Michael. You might notice how Steve has slipped in a shot of each of his three kids holding a cowboy guitar in his book.

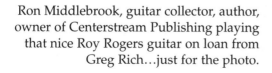

Ron Middlebrook, guitar collector, author, owner of Centerstream Publishing playing that nice Roy Rogers guitar on loan from Greg Rich…just for the photo.

# CONTENTS

# FOREWORD

**W**hen Steve and Ron asked me to write a little bit on the Roy Rogers guitar, many memories came flooding back. I remember these guitars very fondly. I believe I was 7 or 8 when I saw my first Roy Rogers guitar. At that time I had sisters who liked to make my life miserable, so I found it made a great weapon! By wielding the guitar with both hands, and spinning at a high rate of speed, you could take out all the sisters you had before you passed out on the floor in dizzy oblivion! If by chance it was in tune, it made a great musical noise upon contact of the back of your opponent's head! Just kidding, I loved my sisters. Now my brother Sandy, that's another story.

The Roy Rogers guitars brought many hours of enjoyment in our family. Dad would really try hard to teach us all some chords. However, I think he gave up for lack of attention on our part. I did eventually learn to tune a guitar on these less than perfect things. Dad said, "If you work hard at it, you will learn to play. However, you need to want to first."

I have in my collection nearly all of the Roy Rogers guitars listed in this terrific book. I hope you enjoy reading about them again as I did.

Wonderful job Steve and Ron!

*Roy "Dusty" Rogers Jr.*

# PREFACE

A few years ago I received an enthusiastic telephone call from Ron Middlebrook. He had read my "Cowboy Guitars" article in Vintage Guitar Magazine and thought it was a great subject. I already knew about Ron, because his name was shown as publisher on most of the guitar books I had read. He and I came up with a plan to do a "Cowboy Guitars" book together. I would concentrate on the guitar research and he would write the biographies of the cowboys shown on the guitars. As it turned out, Ron was also responsible for gathering information on the new cowboy guitars, like the fabulous models designed by Greg Rich. From the get-go, Ron and I have been on the same wave length and I am more than pleased with how this book has turned out.

I do want to make a few points before we go any further. You'll notice how most of the guitars are tied-in with the mail-order catalogs from Sears, Wards, Spiegel, Eaton's, Simpsons and Sears Canada. These catalogs distributed the lion's share of cowboy guitars, but there were other lesser known outlets for variations of the same guitars. For example, in the 1940's, Sears offered the Gene Autry "Melody Ranch" guitar, but a Gene Autry guitar, without the "Melody Ranch" name, was available as an award for youngsters selling vegetable and flower seeds for The American Seed Company. It should be noted that these variants from other outlets will still generally follow the same time line as the equivalent models sold through the major catalogs.

You will find several of the guitars shown in this book are missing a few guitar strings, and the remaining strings may be black with rust. I favor keeping the rusty strings instead of installing new replacements. Who knows, they might be the original strings and the rust may have been caused by the original owner's perspiration while learning simple country songs like "Little Brown Jug" or "The Crawdad Song" (songs my dad played when he was a boy).

Most cowboy guitars were smaller in size and were simple beginner guitars. Their value today has to do with the art work displayed on them. They come from a time when a youngster's favorite pastime was listening to cowboy radio shows and going to see cowboy movies. Back then, everyone wanted to be just like the hero of the cowboy movies, fighting for what is right and doing all things well, including playing guitar and singing.

As the wooden cowboy guitars were being phased out in the 1950's, fiberboard and plastic cowboy guitars came onto the scene. These were toy instruments and were aimed at an even younger group of kids. This coincides with the advent of cowboy shows on television.

Now in modern times, I am amazed that there are new cowboy guitars available! Jefferson Manufacturing is producing them, and on a higher plane are the high quality cowboy guitars available from companies like Martin, Collings, and Dream Guitars. I think all the cowboy guitars are a lot of fun, and I hope you think they are fun too.

*Steve Evans*

A short overview on distributors and manufacturers of wooden, fiberboard, and plastic cowboy guitars.

## Distributors

Most cowboy guitars were purchased from big mail order catalogs, such as:

1. "Sears, Roebuck & Co." in Chicago, IL (In business from 1886 through present)

2. "Montgomery Ward" in Chicago (1872 through 2001)

3. "Spiegel" in Chicago (1865 through present)

4. "T. Eaton Co." in Toronto, Ontario, Canada (1869 through present)

5. "Simpsons, Limited" in Toronto (pre 1952) "Simpsons-Sears" (1952-1971)

6. "Sears Canada, Inc." in Toronto (1971 through present)

The distributors listed above sold the guitars, but did not make them.

The following lists the names of several manufacturers who made cowboy guitars, and the approximate years they were in business.

## Companies That Have Made Wooden Cowboy Guitars

1. "The Harmony Company" in Chicago, IL (1892 through 1975) Sears, Roebuck & Co. owned Harmony from 1916 through December 1940.

2. "The Kay Musical Instrument Company" in Chicago (1931 through 1969)

3. "Regal" in Chicago (1908 through 1954)

4. "Richter" in Chicago ("Richter" and date stamped inside guitars from 1930-1941)

5. "United" in Jersey City, New Jersey (1940 through 1965)

6. "Holman Luggage Company" in Guelph, Ontario, Canada (1925-1979)

Wooden cowboy guitars have also been produced in Holland, Germany and Australia.

## Companies That Have Made Fiberboard Cowboy Guitars

1. "Jefferson Manufacturing Co." in Philadelphia, PA (1943 through present)

2. "Rich Toy Co." (Range Rhythm Toy) (1924 through 1962) Factories in Tupelo, Mississippi and Chicago, Illinois

## Companies That Have Made Plastic Cowboy Guitars

1. "Mastro Industries, Inc." in Bronx, New York (1950 through late 1960's) Owned by Mario Maccaferri. Sold out the toy instrument division to Carnival in late 1960's.

2. "Mattel Toys" in El Segundo, CA (1945 through present)

3. "Emenee Industries, Inc." in New York City, NY (produced guitars 1955-1968)

4. "The Ohio Art Company" in Bryan, Ohio (1908 through present) Made plastic guitars 1969 through 1991. Purchased Emenee in May of 1968 and moved the injection molding equipment from New York to "Strydel Inc." (a company owned by Ohio Art) in Stryker, Ohio.

5. "Carnival Toys Inc." in Bridgeport, Connecticut (circa 1950's through 1985)

# TIME LINE OF NAMESAKE COWBOY GUITARS

**Bradley Kincaid**
  Houn' Dog......................................................1929-1933

**Carson J. Robison**
  Guitars...........................................................1930-1941
  Uke ................................................................1936-1940

**Gene Autry**
  Round-Up.......................................................1932-1938
  Old Santa Fe, f-hole......................................1935-1936
  Round-Up, no scene ......................................1939-1941
  Melody Ranch ................................................1941-1955
  Silvertone ......................................................1958-1959
  Emenee, plastic with signature ....................1955-1957
  Emenee, without signature ..........................late 1950-1985
  Dream Guitars, Gene Autry Tribute............1998
  Jefferson, fiberboard.....................................2000-present

**Wilf Carter**
  Old style........................................................1935
  New style .......................................................1938 and 1951

**The Lone Ranger**
  Supertone......................................................1936-1941
  Canadian........................................................1937-1950
  Uke.................................................................1939
  Sunburst........................................................1950-1951
  Jefferson, fiberboard
  (3 models) ....................................................1955-1960's
  ......................................................................2001-present

**The Plainsman**
  Guitar ............................................................1938-1943
  Uke.................................................................1939-1940

**Cowboy Loye**
  ......................................................................Circa 1930's

**Ray Whitley**
  ......................................................................1939-1940

**Buck Jones**
  Good Luck, Buck Jones & Silver ..................1940-1943
  Canadian........................................................1940's

**Jerry Smith**
  Regal "Jerry the Yodeling Cowboy"............Circa 1940

**Red Belcher**
  Red Belcher's Favorite ..................................early 1940's

**Louise Massey**
  ......................................................................1941

**Red Foley**
  Smooth Trailin' (2 models)............................early 1940's

**Prairie Ramblers**
  Del Oro...........................................................1942
  Old Kraftsman ...............................................1955-1966

**Jack Lee**
  Powder River, Jack Lee..................................1942-1946

**Bob West**
  ......................................................................Circa 1949

**Kenny Roberts**
  Guitar and Uke..............................................Circa 1950

**Roy Rogers**
  Canadian (2 wood models)............................1951-1958
  Harmony made...............................................1954-1958
  Canadian, plastic ..........................................1957
  Fiberboard, red (2 models)............................1956-1961
  Fiberboard, yellow ........................................1962
  Fiberboard, orange (3 models) .....................1963-1970's
  ......................................................................1999-present
  Dream guitars, Roy & Dale Tributes ............1998

**Tex Morton**
  ......................................................................Circa 1950's

**Lee Moore**
  ......................................................................Circa late 1950's

**Howdy Doody**
  Emenee Uke (at least 2 models) ...................1950's

**Davy Crockett**
  Fiberboard or plastic
  (at least 6 models)........................................Circa late 1950's

**Zorro**
  Emenee, plastic guitar and uke ....................late 1950's
  Canadian, plastic uke....................................late 1950's

**Wyatt Earp**
  Jefferson, fiberboard.....................................1959-1968

**Willie Nelson**
  Carnival, plastic.............................................Circa 1982
  Jefferson, fiberboard.....................................2001-present

**Hopalong Cassidy**
  Jefferson, fiberboard.....................................2000-present

**Riders in the Sky**
  Jefferson, fiberboard.....................................2001-present

OVER there through the shadows
I see a camp fire gleam
And there's a pony grazin'
Beside a peaceful stream.
Is that bacon I smell fryin'?
Yep! and a pot o' coffee too.
And there's a cowboy spreadin' his blanket–
Don't yuh wish you was him? I do!

Carson J. Robison

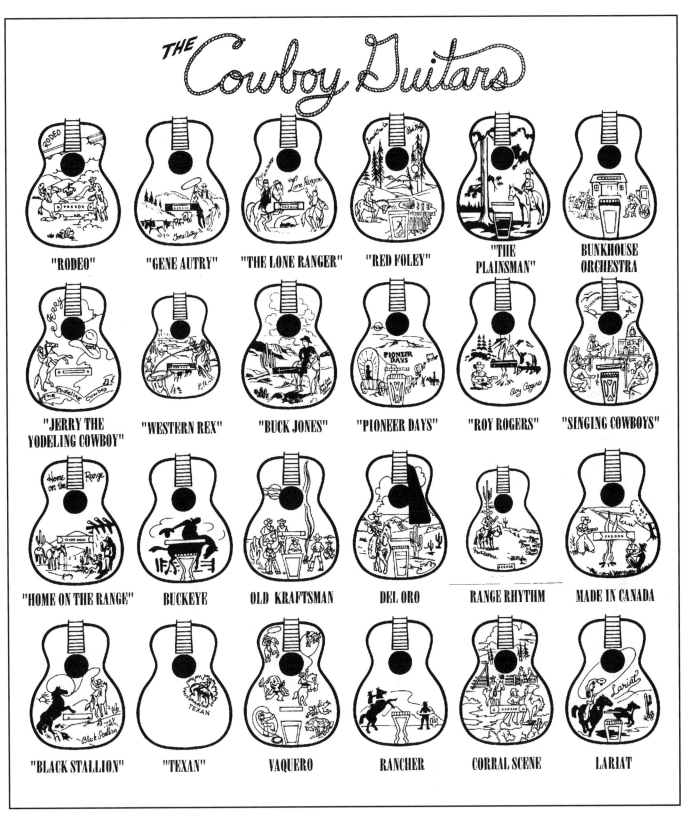

Twenty-four head of the most popular Cowboy stencil guitar designs. Illustration by Toby Isbell; provided courtesy of Steve Evans, Jacksonville (Arkansas) Guitar Center.

# BRADLEY KINCAID "HOUN' DOG" GUITAR

## as Sold by
## Sears, Roebuck & Co.

From the fall of 1929 through the spring of 1933, Sears offered the Bradley Kincaid "Houn' Dog" guitar. This model was made for Sears by the Harmony Company. Sears' advertisement read: "This is the guitar that the well-known radio artist, Bradley Kincaid, uses and which he has named the "Houn' Dog" Guitar. Bradley will help you to learn his favorite selections, which he plays over the radio, as he has agreed to give one of his books with every "Houn' Dog" guitar purchased."

The "Houn' Dog" guitar had a colorful "decalcomania" showing a hound dog in a mountain scene with a reproduction of Bradley Kincaid's signature and the "Houn' Dog" name. The standard size (36 1/2" X 12 3/4") guitar had a clear natural finish. The spruce top had colored-wood-block inlay with white celluloid binding on the top edge and around the soundhole. The mahogany back and sides were also bound with white celluloid. A blue and white "Supertone" paper label was glued inside the guitar and was visible through the soundhole. The V-shaped mahogany neck had a slotted peghead with a Brazilian rosewood overlay. The three-on-a-side tuning machines were brass with black tuning buttons. The flat ebonized fretboard had brass frets and three mother-of-pearl dot inlays. The sculptured rosewood bridge had wooden bridge pins with mother-of-pearl inlays.

**Circa 1929-1933 Bradley Kincaid "Houn' Dog"**, natural finish spruce top with decal showing a hound dog in a mountain scene, rosewood bridge with wooden bridge pins with mother-of-pearl inlaid dots, colorful wood block binding inlays.

**Circa 1929-1933 Bradley Kincaid "Houn' Dog", standard size, 36 1/2" long, slotted peghead, made by Harmony, sold through Sears.**

# BRADLEY KINCAID

Bradley Kincaid (born in Point Leavell, Garrard County, Kentucky, July 13, 1895) lived and grew almost to manhood hidden away in the Kentucky Mountains. He was 19 years old, when he entered the sixth grade in the Foundation department of Berea College, Kentucky. After going to school two years and finishing the sixth, seventh, and eighth grades, Bradley volunteered for army service and spent two years during WWI, one of those years in France. He returned to Berea College at the age of 23 and entered high school. He finished high school at the age of 26. He moved to Chicago and entered the Y.M.C.A. College and was a member of the College Glee Club. It was by accident that the director of the quartet, mentioned to the musical director of WLS that Bradley played and sang the old mountain ballads. He was asked to come to the studio and give a program and the rest is history.

Bradley was the first star on WLS in Chicago, singing folk songs. By 1926 he had become a regular on the WLS Chicago Barn Dance. He remained with the show (later to be known as the National Barn Dance) until 1931. Following graduation in June 1928, Kincaid began touring and at the same time collecting folk songs from a variety of sources, publishing these in a series of songbooks.

His recording career began in 1927, when he made a number of sides for the Gennett record label. These discs appeared on a myriad of other labels, sometimes under a pseudonym. Throughout the '30s and '40s, Kincaid continued to record for Decca and many different labels.

Kincaid was billed as "The Kentucky Mountain Boy with His Houn' Dog Guitar and Old Mountain Songs." (It's told that Bradley's father farmed and raised hound dogs and traded a dog for an old dilapidated guitar to give to Bradley). Kincaid had several top songs such as *Gave My Love A Cherry*, *The Letter Edged In Black*, *Methodist Pie* and *Barbara Allen*, singing the latter over WLS every Saturday night for four successive years. An ever-active radio performer, he bought his own station (WWSO, Springfield, Ohio) in 1949 and sold it in 1953. Besides appearing on nearly every major barn dance. Kincaid played for years in the Northeast, introducing folk and country music to a whole new area before retiring in Springfield. Bradley passed away on September 23, 1989.

**Publicity photo for WLS**

**1941 Songbook**

# "CARSON J. ROBISON" MODEL GUITAR

## as Sold by
## Montgomery Ward

Wards offered Carson J. Robison model guitars from 1930 through 1941. Every year or two the Carson J. Robison guitar had some changes over the previous year's model. The following describes the different variations.

### Variation #1 (Production: Fall 1930 - Fall 1932)

Wards introduced the Carson J. Robison model guitar in the fall of 1930. The Carson J. Robison "Hill Country Outfit" could be ordered for $9.95, postage paid. This outfit included the guitar, neck cord, Hohner Marine Band harmonica with holder ("as used by Carson Robison") and instruction books. This first version had very ornate floral decorations on the front and sides, and had unusual fancy black and white binding on the body and neck. Wards referred to this guitar as "standard" size (36 1/2" X 13 1/4"). The back and sides were made of bird's-eye maple and the top of spruce. This model also had a slotted peghead and no pickguard.

### Variation #2 (Spring 1933)

In the spring of 1933 the Carson J. Robison "Hill Country" was totally changed. Instead of floral decorations, it was painted with a hill country scene. The scene showed a man sitting on a log, playing a guitar to a lady; in the distance a log cabin could be seen. (Note: This scene was used in 1934 on Spiegel's "Mountaineer" guitar and a similar scene appeared on other guitars through 1949) The natural spruce top had a white pearltone pickguard. The body and soundhole were bound in white pyroxylin. The back, sides, and neck were made of mahogany. The pin bridge had a distinctive "canoe" shape. The neck had a slotted peghead and the fretboard was covered with white pearltone.

### Variation #3 (fall1933-fall 1934)

In the fall of 1933 the Carson J. Robison model was no longer called the "Hill Country" and had been drastically changed, again! It was being made in a slightly larger concert size (37 1/2" X 14 3/4") and had no painted decorations or scenes. The spruce top had no pickguard and came in a very dark brown sunburst. All future models would also come in sunburst. The front and back of the body had white binding and the soundhole had white/black/ white binding. The back and sides were made of Honduras mahogany. The mahogany neck joined the body at the 14th fret instead of the 12th fret as on previous models. The fretboard was made of Brazilian rosewood and had five mother-of-pearl position dots. The squared-off, non-slotted peghead had a reproduction of Carson J. Robison's signature.

**Circa 1934 "Carson J. Robison" guitar, dark sunburst finish, spruce top with mahogany back and sides, concert size, 37 1/2" long, 14 frets clear of the body, binding on front and back of body, sold through Wards.**

## Variation #4 (Spring 1935 - Spring 1936)

The Carson J. Robison model of 1935 only had a couple of changes. It still came with binding on the body front, but not on the back, and it now had a pickguard. Besides the normal 6-string model (37 1/2" X 14 3/4"), in the fall of 1935 it could also be ordered as a 4-string tenor guitar (36 1/4" X 14 3/4").

## Variation #5 (Fall 1936 - Fall 1937)

By the fall of 1936, Gibson Guitar Company of Kalamazoo, Michigan, was making the Carson J. Robison model for Wards. It had been enlarged to a grand concert size (40 1/2" X 14 3/4") and the option for the tenor guitar was no longer available. The peghead had been changed to be more shapely than the previous squared style.

## Variation #6 (Spring 1938 - Spring 1939)

The Spring 1938 model's peghead had a small painted-on king's crown, the name "Recording King", the "Carson J. Robison" signature and the designation "Model-K". The types of wood remained the same as the previous five years: eastern spruce top, Honduras mahogany back, sides and neck, and Brazilian rosewood fretboard and bridge. It was available in the grand concert size (40 1/2" X 14 3/4"), but also could be ordered in a 3/4 size guitar (36" X 12 5/8") and in Hawaiian style (38 3/4" X 14 3/4" with high nut and saddle).

**Carson Robison and the Buckaroos**

**Circa 1934 "Carson J. Robison", reproduction of Carson J. Robison signature painted in cream color on squared off peghead.**

## Variation #7 (Fall 1939 - Spring 1940)

In the fall of 1939 the Carson J. Robison model had been changed to a grand auditorium size (41 1/4" X 16 1/4"). The option of ordering as a Hawaiian style (33 3/4" X 14 3/4") was still available, but the 3/4 size had been dropped. With the guitar came the purchaser's choice of three gold colored initials to be applied to the front of the guitar.

## Variation #8 (Fall 1941)

The final variation of the Carson J. Robison model was only offered in the fall of 1941. It had changed to a grand concert size (39 1/2" X 14") and had an oval-shaped soundhole. It also had a reproduction of the Carson Robison signature painted below the bridge. The sunburst body had a spruce top and mahogany back and a tortoise-shell pickguard. The top, soundhole and peghead were bound with black-and-white celluloid binding. The rosewood fretboard had five mother-of-pearl position dots.

1938 "Carson J. Robison" peghead painted with a small crown, "Recording King", a reproduction of Carson's signature and "Model K" designation.

1938 "Carson J. Robison" guitar, brown sunburst, tortoise colored pickguard, grand concert size 40 1/2" long, made by Gibson, sold through Wards.

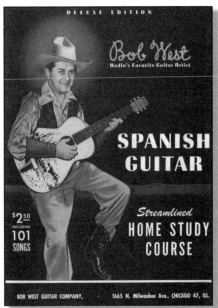

No information can be found on Bob West, "radio's favorite guitar artist." The front and back covers are Bob's but the inside is a Wm. J. Smith Music Co. book, 1947.

1949 "Bob West" peghead with caricature of cowboy sitting on a fence and playing guitar.

Spring of 1949 "Cabin Scene" guitar, "Bob West" name painted on peghead, made by Harmony, natural birch with scene painted in green and orange, this scene is similar to the Carson J. Robison "Hill Country" scene used in the spring of 1933.

The Bob West name is scratched out on the peghead, but Lonnie and Wayne, on the back cover of their 1950 Wm. J. Smith guitar book, say…"this guitar is a sensational value."

# "CARSON J. ROBISON" UKULELE

## as Sold by
## Montgomery Ward

From the fall of 1936 through the spring of 1940, Wards offered the Carson J. Robison model uke. It cost less than $2.00. The birch body had an ebony finish with white celluloid binding around the top edge and soundhole. The body and the art-deco-shaped peghead were painted black, while the whole fretboard was white pearlette, making for a nice contrast in colors. The attractive cowboy scene on the black body was done with white and green paint. The scene showed a cowboy on horseback overlooking a canyon with mountains, trees, and a log cabin visible in the distance. Featured above the scene was a reproduction of Carson J. Robison's signature.

Late 1930's "Carson J. Robison" uke, black finish with scene in white and green, white pearlette fretboard, white binding.

# CARSON J. ROBISON

Born in Oswego, Kansas on August 9, 1890, Carson J. Robison first sang at local functions in the Oswego area. The son of a fiddler and dance caller, he grew up surrounded by music. When old enough to make his own way, Carson tried railroading and oil field work, spending a few years in Tulsa, Oklahoma, where he worked for the Cosden Oil Company. Still, he always returned to music and in 1920, moved to Kansas City, where he became a performer for radio station WDAF. He was one of the first cowboy singers to become a radio performer.

Robison left Kansas City for New York City in 1924, becoming a whistler for Victor; he could whistle two tones in harmony. For four years he also recorded, as guitarist and co-vocalist, with Vernon Dalhart, the first successful country/western recording artist. By the late 1920's his NBC radio appearances as a cowboy singer along with his recording successes made him nationally famous. After the termination of the Dalhart association, Robinson formed another duo – with Frank Luther (Francis Luther Crowe) whose voice resembled Dalhart's.

As a songwriter, Robison used many themes, including cowboys and the West. He wrote the ever-popular *Carry Me Back to the Lone Prairie*, plus *Barnacle Bill the Sailor*, *Open Up Them Pearly Gates*, *Little Green Valley*, *Blue Ridge Mountain Home*, and *Left My Gal In the Mountains*. In all he wrote over three hundred songs, including his 1948 hit *Life Gets Tee-jus, Don't It?* Five songbooks (probably more) were issued using songs he recorded and/or wrote. Each was illustrated as a cowboy songbook.

Robison recorded for many companies: RCA, Conqueror, Supertone and others using at least nine pseudonyms. He also headed several bands: The Buckaroos, The Carson Robison Trio, the Pioneers, and the Pleasant Valley Boys. Based in Pleasant Valley, New York, during the 1940s and 1950s, Robison remained an active performer and writer until his death on March 24, 1957. One of his final MGM recordings was a rockabilly track, *Rockin' And Rollin' With Grandmaw*. He was a creative songwriter who loved the romance of the West.

**1930 Songbook**

**Publicity photo**

# GENE AUTRY "ROUNDUP" GUITAR
## as Sold by
## Sears, Roebuck & Co

From the fall of 1932 through the fall of 1938 Sears offered the Gene Autry "Roundup" guitar. This model was produced by the Harmony Company for Sears and was the first stencil-painted cowboy guitar offered by Sears. When first introduced in the fall of 1932, the "Roundup" cost $9.75. It had a natural finished spruce top, mahogany back and sides, and a mahogany neck. The body was 12 3/4" wide at the lower bout, 7" at the waist and 9 1/8" at the upper bout. The total length of the guitar was 36 3/8" and was referred to as "standard size". The top and back edges of the body and the soundhole had a four-layer white and black binding.

The word "Round-Up" and a small caricature of a cowboy on horseback were painted on the slotted peghead. The tuning machines were brass plank style with black tuning buttons. The guitar's most remarkable feature was the top, which was painted with an attractive Western scene, showing a cattle roundup and a cowboy on horseback swinging a lariat above his head. At the bottom of the scene, a reproduction of Gene Autry's signature could be seen. By the fall of 1933 the measurements had been slightly changed: 13" wide at the lower bout, 8" at the waist, 9 3/8" at the upper bout by 35 7/8" in total length.

Sears' 1932 fall catalog heralds the introduction of the Gene Autry "Round-up" guitar. This was before Gene Autry had begun his movie career-he went on to start a "Singing Cowboy" phenomenon in the movies. The "Round-up" guitar was the first stencil-painted "Cowboy Guitar" and created quite a stir in the guitar market. Note end-opening canvas case.

In the fall of 1934 the feature of binding on the back had been discontinued and the back and sides that had been mahogany were being made of birch. The changes were reflected by the lower price of $8.25. At about the same time, the fretboard was made with four mother-of-pearl dot inlays compared to three dots previously. In the fall of 1935 a larger "concert size" was introduced. The new version was 14" wide at the lower bout, 8 5/8" at the waist, 10 1/8" at the upper bout by 39" in total length.

The "concert size" had the modern improvement of a longer scale neck having 14 frets clear of the body. In 1936 the natural finish was phased out; the spruce top was changed to a dark shaded finish. The "Round-Up" with its Western cowboy scene was produced up until the fall of 1938 and then was discontinued. However, the same striking western scene would show up a few years later on the Gene Autry "Melody Ranch" model.

**Attractive Supertone label with an oval "F32" date stamp inside a Gene Autry "Round-up" model guitar.**

**Fall of 1932 Gene Autry "Round-up", the original stencil-painted cowboy guitar, natural finish with cowboy scene painted in orange and brown.**

*"It was a brand new Gene Autry guitar with a horse and lariat on the front,"* George recalls. *"I took it home and it hardly ever left my hands. Note by note, I learned to play it. I've owned countless expensive guitars in my life, but none of them ever meant any more to me than that little Gene Autry model."...*

George Jones, "Country Weekly" magazine, March 2, 1999

Another fall of 1932 "Round-Up",
standard size 36 3/8" long, spruce top and mahogany
back and sides with real binding on front and back.

Fall of 1934 Gene Autry "Round-Up", 4 mother-of-pearl inlaid position dots, spruce top with birch back and sides, scene painted in tan and brown.

**Spring of 1935 Gene Autry "Round-up",
made by Harmony and sold through Sears.**

**Closeup of peghead of fall of
1934 Gene Autry "Round-up".**

Fall of 1936 Gene Autry "Round-up", concert size in dark shaded (sunburst) finish, scene painted in brown and orange.

Fall of 1935 Gene Autry, large concert size "Round-up", 39" long, 14 frets clear of the body, natural spruce top with scene painted in orange and brown.

1936 Movie poster

Body shot of a 1936 concert size Gene Autry "Round-up".

Rare photo of Gene in front of the camera.

Big rectangle blue and silver Supertone label inside a fall of 1936 Gene Autry "Round-up".

# GENE AUTRY "OLD SANTA FE" ARCH TOP GUITAR

## As sold by
## Sears, Roebuck & Co.

From the fall of 1935 through the spring of 1936, Sears offered the Gene Autry "Old Santa Fe" model guitar. This model was made for Sears by the Harmony Company. Sears touted, "Gene Autry selected this model as the best for his screen and radio work".

The "Old Santa Fe" was a super auditorium (40 1/2" X 15 3/4") arch-top guitar with 'f' holes. A reproduction of Gene Autry's signature was painted in white on the lower left bout just below the 'f' hole. The guitar was finished in a violin-like sunburst. The top was made of spruce and the back and sides made of figured maple. The body and fretboard were bound with white ivaroid. An elongated black pickguard with white edging was mounted to the top. The strings attached to a nickel-plated trapeze tailpiece and crossed over a moveable adjustable bridge. The steel-reinforced neck had an oval ebonized fretboard with six mother-of-pearl inlaid position dots. The long scale neck had fourteen frets clear of the body. The guitar body did not have a scene, but the peghead had a small scene, painted in white, showing a church with the name "Old Santa Fe" just below.

**Fall of 1935 "Old Santa Fe", super auditorium size arch top 40 1/2" long, sunburst finish, Gene Autry signature on body.**

**Closeup of peghead of fall of 1935 "Old Santa Fe", Gene Autry guitar.**

# GENE AUTRY "ROUND-UP" GRAND CONCERT GUITAR

## as Sold by

## Sears, Roebuck & Co.

From the spring of 1939 through the spring of 1941, Sears offered the Gene Autry "Round-Up" grand concert (15" X 39 1/4") guitar. This big guitar was made by the Harmony Company for Sears.

This model was totally different from the 1932-1938 Gene Autry "Round-Up". It had a spruce top with maple back and sides, finished in a reddish brown sunburst and had black/white/black celluloid binding around the soundhole and on the top and back edges of the body. It also had a tortoise-colored pickguard and a stationary pin bridge. The neck had fourteen frets clear of the body and had a rosewood-colored fretboard with six mother-of-pearl position dots. There was no western scene painted on the body, but a big reproduction of Gene Autry's signature was painted in white on the fretboard. On the slotted peghead, a small caricature of a cowboy on horseback with the name "Round-Up" was painted in white (same peghead scene as '32-'38 "Round-Up").

**1939 Gene Autry grand concert size "Round-up", spruce top with maple back and sides, reddish brown sunburst, just below the bridge are three pick shaped initials of the original owner "SWB"; these decals came with the guitar when it was new.**

**Gene Autry signature stencil painted in white on fretboard of circa 1939-1941 grand concert "Round-Up", same caricature on peghead as the painted scene "Round-Up" of the early 1930's.**

Circa 1939-1941 "Round-up" grand concert size
guitar (15" X 39 1/4"), 14 frets clear of body,
sunburst with tortoise colored pickguard.

# GENE AUTRY "MELODY RANCH" GUITAR

## as sold by

## Sears, Roebuck & Co.

From the fall of 1941 through the spring of 1955, Sears offered the Gene Autry "Melody Ranch" guitar. This model was made for Sears by the Harmony Company. The Western scene "Round-Up" had been gone from the line for three years, but there were still plenty of young Gene Autry fans desiring such an instrument. In the fall of 1941 Sears unveiled the Gene Autry "Melody Ranch".

**Round blue and silver small Supertone label and "S42" date stamp inside 3/4 size 1942 "Melody Ranch".**

The new model had the same western cowboy scene and signature as did the "Round-Up", but the peghead was now painted with a new western motif showing a sign post that read "Melody Ranch". The bound spruce top had a shaded walnut (sunburst) finish as did the maple back and sides. For the first years Sears offered personalized gold initialing to be applied on the lower left-hand side of the guitar. The oval ebonized fretboard had 18 frets (12 clear of the body) and four mother-of-pearl dot inlays. The guitar came in two sizes: standard size (13 1/8" X 35 3/4") and 3/4 size (11 1/8" X 32"). Costing the same as the standard size, the 3/4 size was advertised as intended for small children or ladies. After one year the 3/4 size was dropped leaving one choice, the standard size.

**Spring of 1942 Gene Autry "Melody Ranch", small 3/4 size 32" long, sunburst spruce top with maple back and sides, scene painted in cream and brown.**

**Early 1940's "Melody Ranch", standard size 35 3/4" long, has small round Supertone label inside and pre-war real mother-of-pearl position dots.**

Production and sales were good until 1943. The escalation of World War II found virtually all factories making munitions in support of the war effort. Guitar manufacturing ground to a halt. Production of the "Melody Ranch" did not get back in gear until 1945. Beginning in 1945 the dot inlays on the guitar's fretboard were no longer real mother-of-pearl, but were an imitation made of celluloid (pearloid).

In 1950 the good old shaded brown "Melody Ranch" had been changed to glossy black and the fretboard now had painted-on white block-style markers. The black model was only offered one year and in mid-1951 the finish was changed to a glossy shaded brown (although still with white block markers), and that is how it remained until production ceased in 1955.

**Sears 1944 spring catalog proclaims "In it for the duration!", no appliances available – no guitars either.**

**Sears 1943 fall catalog showed the effects of World War II in progress.**

Late 1940's Gene Autry peghead shows a sign post that reads "Melody Ranch".

Body shot of late 1940's Gene Autry "Melody Ranch". The "Melody Ranch" used the same scene as its predecessor the Gene Autry "Round-up".

Late 1940's "Melody Ranch", with post-war imitation mother-of-pearl position dots.

Early 1950's Gene Autry guitar, no
"Melody Ranch" name on peghead,
Harmony factory second, with
Western Music Company label,
not sold through Sears.

Western Music Co. label inside
early 1950's Gene Autry guitar.

WESTERN MUSIC CO.
All Types of Guitars — Lessons
Phone FR. 2-3949
2671 N. TEUTONIA AVE.
MILWAUKEE, WIS.

Circa 1950 Gene Autry guitar with no
"Melody Ranch" name on peghead,
made by Harmony, but not sold by
Sears, all birch body, light-colored
sunburst with reverse scene colors.

1939, Gene on Champion, traveled in style.

1954 Gene Autry "Melody Ranch",
sunburst with painted on
block position markers.

1950 rare glossy black "Melody
Ranch", painted on block position
markers and bound fretboard.

# SILVERTONE
## as Sold by
## Sears, Roebuck & Co

From the fall of 1958 through Christmas of 1959, Sears offered a small 3/4 size Silvertone guitar using the same scene as the Gene Autry model, minus Autry's signature. This model was made by the Harmony Company for Sears. The 3/4 size (11 1/2" X 32 1/4") had a burgundy stained finish with the scene painted in red and cream colors. White striping was painted on the top edge and around the soundhole. The top was made of birch and the back was made of maple. While the top, sides and neck had the burgundy finish, the guitar back had a brown sunburst effect.

The fretboard was stained dark brown with four inlaid position dots and brass frets, and the string nut was made of wood. The Silvertone brand name was painted in white on the peghead. The plank style tuning keys had brass posts and gears with white tuning buttons. The ebonized pinless bridge had a piece of brass fret wire for a saddle and was secured with two Phillips screws. This bridge was the same style that had been used on the wooden Roy Rogers models. This little guitar is attractive, but is one of the more common "Cowboy Guitars". Considering that this model was offered for a period of only one year, we have to assume that it was produced in great number.

1959 Silvertone.

**Close-up of peghead of fall of 1959 "Silvertone" made by Harmony and sold by Sears.**

**Fall of 1959 "Silvertone", Gene Autry style scene, small 3/ 4 size 32 1/ 4" long, burgundy finish with scene in cream and red.**

# GENE AUTRY COWBOY GUITAR
## Plastic Child's Guitar

In the year 1955 only, Montgomery Ward offered the "Gene Autry" child's guitar, and only in 1956, Spiegel offered the same model. It was a 3/4 size (32" X 11") guitar made by Emenee Industries of New York who specialized in making plastic musical instruments and toys.

The entire guitar was made of plastic with the exception of the black metal tailpiece and the tuning gears. It was a tenor (four string) model and came stock with one plastic and three metal strings. Several raised Western decorations were molded into the guitar top, including a Western belt encircling the sound hole, Gene Autry sitting on a fence playing guitar, a six-shooter with holster, a steer, Gene Autry riding a horse, Gene Autry's face, a steer's skull, a boot spur and Gene Autry's signature.

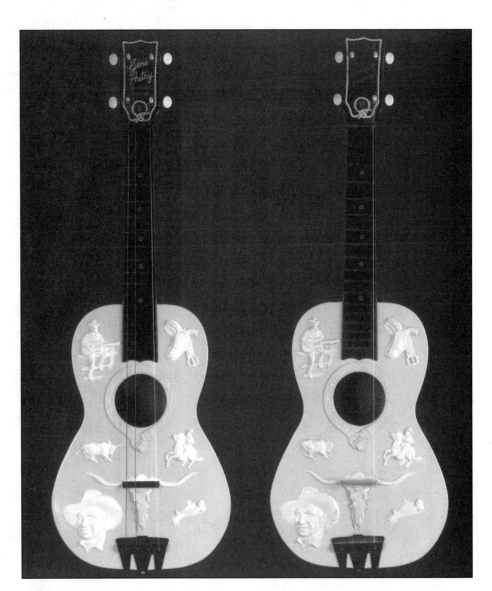

**1955 Gene Autry "Cowboy Guitar", four string plastic guitar with raised cowboy scenes molded into the top, made by Emenee Industries in New York.**

**Late 1950's Emenee "Cowboy Guitar", tan-colored four string plastic guitar, same as Gene Autry model, but without signature.**

The guitar top was tan with most of the reliefs painted in a putty color. The back of the body and neck were a swirling tan color, while the front of the neck was black. The fretboard had five red dot position markers with the letters "EM" inside each dot. The black peghead showed the brand "Emenee", a reproduction of Gene Autry's signature and the name "Cowboy Guitar" all encircled by a white rope.

Even though it was toy-like, the plastic "Gene Autry" was an actual working guitar intended for children to learn on. It came with a neck cord, instruction book, pick and an alligator embossed cardboard case with a picture of Gene Autry on it. Also included was a chord player device; when attached to the fretboard, it would automatically make chords as the appropriate buttons were depressed.

Emenee Industries' small 16-page catalog showing the Gene Autry guitar, Authur Godfrey uke, plus a saxophone, trombone, tuba, banjo, and other musical intruments.

**Early 1960's Emenee "Hootenanny Guitar", bright white six string plastic guitar.**

**Peghead of early 1960's Emenee "Hootenanny Guitar" with plastic friction tuning pegs.**

# Later Versions with Same Scenes without the Gene Autry Name

In the late 1950's Emenee produced a "Cowboy Guitar" model identical in features and colors to the "Gene Autry", but it no longer had the Gene Autry signature on it. By the early 1960's this model had changed to a six string guitar with the name "Hootenanny Guitar" painted on the peghead. The front of the body and the reliefs were all one color-bright white. The back was black with white swirls. The tuning keys were white plastic and were friction style. By 1963 the name on the peghead had changed to "Western Guitar", but by 1964 this model had been dropped from the line.

From the early 1970's through 1985, Emenee offered another six-string plastic guitar with the same raised Western scenes as the previous models mentioned, but the model name was called "Western Folk".
This guitar was actually produced by the Ohio Art Company who had purchased the Emenee name and the plastic molding equipment and moved it all to their plant in Stryker, Ohio, in 1969. The "Western Folk" has the same cowboy designs as the previous models, but the name "Western Folk" was painted on the body where the raised "Gene Autry" name had been on the original 1955 model. The colors were different from the old models too. The guitar had a putty-colored top with a chocolate brown back and neck, and the reliefs were painted in chocolate brown and bone white. The tailpiece had changed in color from black to brushed-aluminum silver or gold. The fretboard position dots were large and shiny gold in color. The diminutive plastic tuning keys were unusual in that they had tuning gear mechanisms concealed inside the peghead.

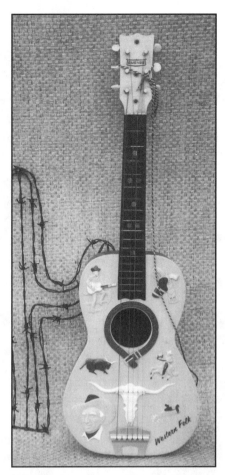

**Circa 1970's Emenee "Western Folk", putty colored six string plastic guitar, with a gold colored aluminum tailpiece.**

**Three different Emenee plastic guitars, a 1970's "Western Folk", 1955 "Gene Autry" with original box, and a late 1950's "Cowboy Guitar".**

1963 Emenee "Western Guitar" with raised western decorations molded into the bright white top, showing a western belt encircling the soundhole, cowboy's (Gene Autry's) face, a steer, cowboy sitting on fence playing guitar, a six shooter with holster, cowboy riding a horse, a steers skull and a boot spur.

1981 Emenee "Western Folk" guitar, mint condition in its box with original song/instruction book and a triangle black pick, made by Ohio Art, this one has a silver colored aluminum tailpiece.

1938 Movie poster

# GENE AUTRY

Orvon Gene Autry's career in the entertainment industry spanned sixty years. He was known as "America's Favorite Singing Cowboy," and is the only entertainer to have five stars on Hollywood's Walk of Fame…for radio, records, film, television, and live theatrical performance. Gene was born in Tioga, Texas, September 29, 1907, with cowboy blood in his veins. His father was a horse trader and livestock dealer. His mother, Elnora, taught him to play guitar, and his grandfather, a reverend at Indian Creek Baptist Church, had him sing in the church choir. At age 12, with eight dollars and a Sears-Roebuck catalogue, Autry acquired his first guitar.

In the late 1920s, Gene began his rise from a $150-a-month guitar-playing singer and songwriting-railroad telegrapher to Hollywood superstar.

According to legend, Gene was singing and playing in the office one night working the graveyard shift as a railroad telegrapher, when he met Will Rogers who, after hearing Autry sing, encouraged him to seek a professional career. Gene took off for New York to make the rounds of recording companies. He was advised to get some experience singing on radio to polish his skill.

Back to Tulsa he went and worked at radio station KVOO. A year later he returned to New York and signed with the American Recording Company (later Columbia Records). In 1929, his first recording covered Jimmie Rodgers' standards so closely that many listeners thought it was Rodgers.

His rocket to stardom came in 1931 with the recording hit, co-written with his railroad singing buddy Jimmie Long, "That Silver Haired Daddy of Mine." That landed him on the famous WLS *National Barn Dance* radio program in Chicago and not long after he had his own show on WLS.

Hollywood was calling. In 1934 he got a singing cowboy part in the Ken Maynard western, *In Old Santa Fe*. Next was a staring role in the cowboy-science-fiction 12 part serial, *The Phantom Empire*, which led to his first starring western role in *Tumbling Tumbleweeds*, the first of his 93 movies with sidekicks Smiley Burnette and Pat Buttram.

In 1938, he held out for a new contract from Republic, and that occasion opened the door for Roy Rogers to enter the scene, as Republic's other singing cowboy star.

Gene served in the United States Army Air Force as a flight officer from 1943 until 1945, toured with a USO troupe and resumed his movie career in 1946.

Of the 635 recordings he made, he wrote or co-wrote more than 300. Gene's recordings have sold more than 60 million copies with more that a dozen gold records. "Rudolph the Red-Nosed Reindeer" (1949) is the second best selling single of all time. The *Gene Autry's Melody Ranch* was heard weekly over the CBS Radio Network between 1940 and 1956. In 1950 he moved to television producing and starring in 91 half-hour episodes of *The Gene Autry Show*, still shown today on the Western Channel. He finally hung up his performance spurs in 1956.

Gene's accomplishments and business successes are far too many to even attempt to mention in this short tribute as he was one of California's most successful businessmen, even purchasing the California Angels baseball team in 1961.

The town of Gene Autry, Oklahoma was renamed after him with its own Gene Autry museum.

On October 2, 1998, Gene headed off into his last sunset, but his legacy will continue to live on in the hearts of his fans and in the museum he founded in 1988. The Autry Museum of Western Heritage (visit www.autry-museum.org) in Los Angeles is considered one of the finest museums of the American West.

**Trivia:** In the late 1920s and early 1930s, Autry records were issued on different labels under these pseudonyms: John Hardy, Sam Hill, Tom Long, Overton Hatfield, Gene Johnson, Jimmie Smith, Bob Clayton, Johnny Dodds, and The Long Brothers (with Jimmy Long). In addition, Autry played guitar accompaniment on four George Gobel recordings on April 12, 1933.

**More trivia:** In 1933 he ordered the first Martin 12-fret D-45. (Martin recreated that same guitar in 1994 with 66 guitars individually numbered and signed by Gene and C.F. Martin IV) some of his other guitars were: Martin 000-45, Pearl-trimmed Euphonon (Larson Brothers), and two custom-built Gibson Super Jumbos.

# "LEFTY COWBOY ON HORSE" GUITAR

## as sold by
## Spiegel

From Christmas 1934 through the spring of 1944 (as a "Del Oro"), and again in the spring of 1950 (as an "Old Kraftsman"), Spiegel offered a guitar with a scene showing a cowboy on horseback strumming a guitar left-handed. This model was made by the Kay Musical Instrument Company for Spiegel. The scene's cowboy resembled Gene Autry wearing chaps and a big cowboy hat. Also shown were cacti, a mountain range and clouds. Three pick-shaped decals with the purchaser's initials were included with the guitar through 1942. When introduced (1934 Christmas season), the "Lefty Cowboy" scene guitar came in a very attractive blond (cream colored) finish, with scene painted in brown. A matching brown stripe was painted around the top edge of the body, peghead and soundhole. The name "Del Oro" was painted in brown on the squared-off blond peghead. The ebonized fretboard had four mother-of-pearl inlaid position dots and eighteen frets (twelve clear of the body). The guitar was made of birch and was standard size (37" X 13 1/4"). It had a nickel plated trapeze tailpiece with a moveable wooden bridge.

**Early 1940's Del Oro "Lefty Cowboy on Horse" scene, grand concert size 36 3/4" long, tortoise colored pickguard.**

**Circa 1941 Del Oro, scene shows a left-handed singing cowboy riding a horse, blond (cream) colored guitar with brown scene, note on upper right of body are original owner's initials on pick shaped decals.**

Spiegel didn't offer the "Lefty Cowboy" guitar from the fall of 1935 through the spring of 1939. It reappeared in the 1939 catalog in a light-brown sunburst finish with a gold colored scene. By the spring of 1941 the finish had changed back to the blond finish with a brown scene like the 1934 model. In the fall of 1941 and spring of 1942 the "Lefty Cowboy" guitar had again disappeared from the Spiegel catalog, but was back in the lineup for the fall of 1942. The fall 1942 model was changed to a larger "grand concert" size (36 3/4" X 14 1/2") and was now coming with a pickguard that was attached with two slot-head wood screws. The guitar was finished in brown sunburst with the scene and striping painted in white. Spiegel advertised the guitar as "sells in most music stores for $11.00, Spiegel's price $6.75". For $2.00 more, one could also receive a plaid colored cotton fiber carrying bag along with several accessories, including Spanish and Hawaiian books, four picks, slide bar, extension nut, neck cord and three initials.

**Close-up of peghead of early 1940's "Del Oro".**

**Early 1940's Del Oro "Lefty Cowboy on Horse" scene, brown sunburst with scene and striping painted in white, note three pick shaped decals are the original owner's initials "O.S.B."**

By the fall of 1943 the trapeze tailpiece had been slightly changed. The new version had visible string slots, differing from the previous trapeze that had its string attachment hidden on the underside of the tailpiece. Missing from the line from the fall of 1944 through the fall of 1949, the "Lefty Cowboy" showed up one last time for the 1950 spring catalog. Instead of being called a "Del Oro", it had the "Old Kraftsman" name painted on the peghead. It had the same scene and coloring as the previous model, but the measurements had slightly changed (37 3/4" X 13 3/4"), and it did not have a pickguard. The fretboard now had fourteen frets clear of the body and the nickel plated tailpiece was now solid with a raised area in the center instead of an opening.

Early 1940's Del Oro "Lefty Cowboy on Horse" scene, brown sunburst with white scene, black triangular pickguard, made by Kay sold through Spiegel.

Circa 1950 Old Kraftsman "Lefty Cowboy on Horse" scene, sunburst with white scene, 37 3/4" long, 14 frets clear of the body.

# "HILL BILLY BAND" SCENE GUITAR
## as Sold by
## Montgomery Ward

From the fall of 1935 through the fall of 1936, Wards offered the "Hill Billy Band" scene guitar. The scene, "Created by Ward's Bureau of Design", was described in Ward's catalog as "Hill-billys playing their mountain music". The scene showed five musicians playing instruments: harmonica, fiddle, clarinet, guitar and an accordion. The guitar's all birch body was painted with black lacquer and the scene painted in black and white. The neck had a slotted peghead and an ebonized fretboard with three inlaid position dots. The guitar had a nickel plated trapeze style tailpiece with moveable wood bridge. The "standard size" guitar measured 36 1/4" in total length and 13 1/2" at the lower bout. In the fall of 1936 the peghead was slightly changed with contour cuts giving an art deco look.

The "Hill Billy Band" scene guitar came with a braided neck cord, instruction book and a pick for only $3.95. For an additional 30 cents the outfit would also include a Hawaiian instruction book, thumb pick and two finger picks, steel bar, and an extension nut to raise the strings for Hawaiian style playing.

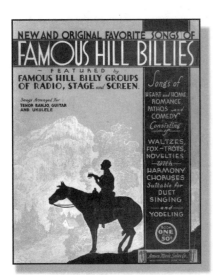

**1934 Songbook**

Circa 1935 "Hill Billy Band" scene guitar, slotted peghead, all birch body, trapeze tailpiece, sold through Ward's.

Wards label inside a circa 1935 "Hill Billy Band" scene guitar.

Circa 1935 "Hill Billy Band" scene, black guitar with scene painted in black and white.

# OLD STYLE "WILF CARTER" GUITAR

## as Sold by

## T. Eaton Company

## (Made in Canada)

For the fall of 1935, Eaton's offered a "Wilf Carter" model guitar. Wilf Carter, "The Yodeling Cowboy", also known as "Montana Slim", was a well known Canadian radio and recording artist. This standard size (36 3/4" X 13") birch guitar was painted all black and had a three color (blue, cream & red) cowboy scene on the body. The scene showed three cowboys around a campfire – one on the left is standing and playing a guitar, and two on the right are sitting on the ground with one of them playing a uke – a tree can be seen in the background. At the lower left portion of the scene was a reproduction of Wilf Carter's signature. The guitar had white binding inlaid around the top edge, soundhole and fretboard. The pin bridge and fretboard were ebonized, and three white position dots were inlaid on the fretboard. The peghead was slotted and was very squared off. This guitar was also sold through a distributor other than Eaton, who offered a model with the same scene, but no "Wilf Carter" signature and no white binding.

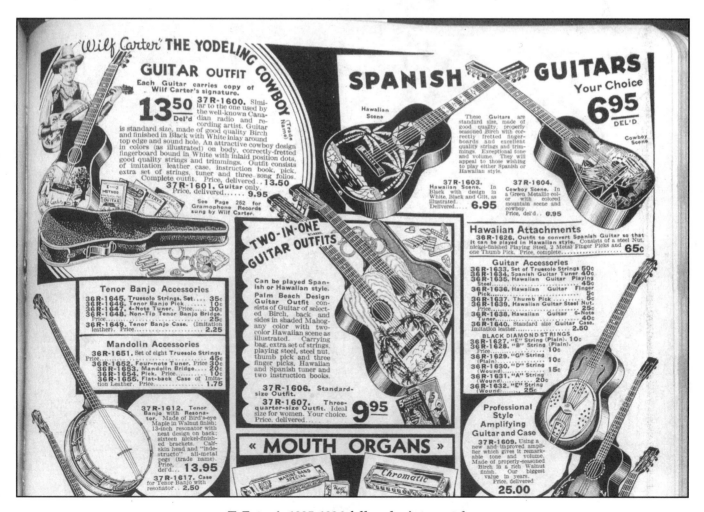

**T. Eaton's 1935-1936 fall and winter catalog
shows the "old style" "Wilf Carter" guitar.**

T. Eaton used the cover art from Smith's 1932 Songbook on the "Wilf Carter" model guitar below.

Circa fall of 1935 "Wilf Carter" model guitar, standard size 36 3/4" long , pin bridge, slotted peghead, three inlaid position dots.

Circa fall of 1935 "Wilf Carter" model, black with scene painted in blue, cream and red, "Made in Canada" rubber stamped inside the soundhole.

# THE NEW STYLE "WILF CARTER" GUITAR

## as Sold by

## T. Eaton Company

For the fall of 1938, Eaton's introduced a new "Wilf Carter" model guitar. The standard size (36 1/2" X 13 1/4") guitar had a mahogany stained birch back and sides with a natural finished spruce top. The scene was painted in orange and black and showed a cowboy (Wilf Carter), wearing a big cowboy hat, playing a guitar while sitting beneath a big tree, which was positioned on the left side of the guitar and extended the length of the body.

On the lower right was a campfire, and up above and to the right of the sound hole was a reproduction of Wilf Carter's signature. Features that were the same as the old style "Wilf Carter" model included white binding around the top edge, soundhole and fretboard; ebonized pin bridge and an ebonized fretboard with three dot inlays; and a squared off slotted peghead.

1939 Songbook

1935 Songbook by Wilf Carter, the photo of Wilf was used for the art scene on the top of the guitars. Notice the same pose, vest and hat.

# THE NEW STYLE "WILF CARTER" GUITAR

## as Sold by

## Simpsons Limited

For the spring of 1951, Simpson's offered a "Wilf Carter" model guitar. It had the same scene as the 1938 "Wilf Carter" sold by Eaton, but had several changes. It no longer had the "Wilf Carter" signature and did not have binding. The guitar no longer came with a spruce top, but instead was all birch. Instead of a stationary pin bridge, it had a metal trapeze tailpiece with a moveable wooden bridge, and instead of a slotted peghead, it had the more modern looking solid peghead.

**Circa spring of 1951 new style "Wilf Carter" model, natural birch top with mahogany stained birch back and sides, nickel plated trapeze tailpiece, solid peghead, three position dots, as sold by Simpsons.**

**Circa spring of 1951 "Wilf Carter" model guitar, natural finish, scene in orange and black shows Wilf also known as "Montana Slim" sitting under a tree and playing a guitar.**

# WILF CARTER

A real pioneer of Canadian country music, Wilf Carter, the son of a Baptist minister, was born in Port Hilford, Nova Scotia in 1904. At an early age he was inspired by the performance of a Swiss yodeler and developed his own three-in-one, or echo yodel, a trademark of his performance. In 1923 he was hired by Calgary radio station CFCN to sing on their weekly hoedowns.

In the early '30s he recorded an audition demo of *Swiss Moonlight Lullaby* and *The Capture of Albert Johnson*, which RCA victor released in 1933. It was a bestseller and helped RCA from going bankrupt during the Depression. Carter went to New York after landing his own CBS radio show. When a young woman who was typing out his songs gave him the name Montana Slim, it stuck.

Throughout his long career as a singer-songwriter-guitarist, spanning six decades, he cut more than 40 albums for Bluebird, Decca, Starday, RCA and others and had several music books. He was inducted into the Canadian music hall of fame in 1985 and recorded his last album, *Whatever Happened to all Those Years*, in 1988.

Wilf was 91 when he passed away on December 5th 1996 at his home in Scottsdale, Arizona.

# VAQUERO "RODEO SCENE" GUITAR
## as Sold by
## Spiegel

In 1936 Spiegel offered a "Rodeo Scene" guitar. It was only available for the one year. This model was made for Spiegel by the Kay Musical Instrument Company, and it had the name "Vaquero" painted on the Gibson shaped peghead. The scenes were painted in red and white on the guitar top. Six cowboys were shown doing rodeo activities; one was twirling a lariat above his head while riding a horse, one was on horseback lassoing a steer, one was being thrown from a bucking bronc, one was doing rope tricks and one was wrestling a steer. The detail, color and the action shown in the art work make this cowboy guitar very intriguing.

**1936 peghead of the "Rodeo Scene" guitar, "Vaquero" name painted in white on Gibson shaped peghead.**

**1936 Vaquero "Rodeo Scene" guitar, standard size 36 1/4" long.**

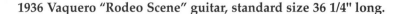

The guitar was a standard size (36 1/4" X 13 1/2") with body made of birch. The finish was a plum colored sunburst with white striping around the soundhole and top edge. The nickel plated trapeze tailpiece, typical of this era, had string attachment hidden from view and a moveable wooden bridge. The V-shaped neck had eighteen frets (twelve clear of the body) and an ebonized fretboard with four mother-of-pearl dot inlays.

Spiegel's price of $4.98 must have seemed very reasonable, even for 1936, especially with all the accessories included with the guitar – a silk neck cord, thumb pick, two finger picks, Hawaiian extension nut, steel slide bar, two instruction books (Spanish and Hawaiian), and the three initials of the guitar's owner in gold leaf.

**1936 Vaquero "Rodeo Scene" guitar, plum colored sunburst with scenes painted in red and white, made by Kay, sold through Spiegel.**

# "COWBOY LASSOING SOUNDHOLE" UKE

## as Sold by
## Montgomery Ward

The fall of 1936 was the only time Wards offered this model. This standard size 21" X 7" uke had a body made of birch finished in a walnut shaded sunburst. The scene painted in cream colored paint showed a cowboy on horseback with his lasso going up and around the soundhole. In the distance was another cowboy on horseback, a cactus, and a mountain range. A white stripe encircles the edge of the soundhole.

The dark brown neck had twelve brass frets with three inlaid position dots. The black button tuning keys were the "non-slip" type with an adjustment screw on each. With quality features like the good tuners and "kerfed lining" inside the body, this ukulele must have been an exceptional value at only 98 cents.

**Circa fall of 1936 "Cowboy Lassoing Soundhole" uke, walnut shaded sunburst with scene in white, standard size, 21" long.**

**1920's Photo from Wyoming showing cowboys playing ukulele, harmonica and guitar.**

# "COWBOY AND COWGIRL AGAINST FENCE" UKE

## as Sold by
## Montgomery Ward

From the fall of 1936 through the spring of 1937, Wards offered the "cowboy and cowgirl against fence" scene model. This standard size (21" X 7") uke had a body made of birch and was finished in a dark mahogany color. The Western scene showed a cowboy and a cowgirl leaning against a fence. White striping was painted around the soundhole and the top edge of the body. The peghead had the same sculptured shape as the "Carson J. Robison" uke being produced at the same time. The tuning pegs were the non-slip type with adjuster screws. The same scene appeared on a gray colored uke with scene in black; however, the gray model was not available from Ward's.

**Arizona Highways magazine cover,
September 1948**

**This gray colored uke has the same scene as a dark brown model sold by Wards from the fall of 1936 through the spring of 1937.**

# THE "LONE RANGER" GUITAR

## as Sold by

## Sears, Roebuck & Co.

From the fall of 1936 through the spring of 1941, Sears offered the "Lone Ranger" guitar. This model was made for Sears by the Harmony Company. It was available in two sizes: standard size (36" X 13 1/2") and 3/4 size (32 1/2" X 11 1/4"). In observation of other cowboy guitar models that came in the two sizes, the smaller of the two would typically be missing a portion of the scene, but in the case of the "Lone Ranger" proportionally sized stencils were used to allow the whole scene to fit on both sizes of this guitar model. In 1936 Sears offered either size for $4.25 with an additional $1.40 charge for an optional canvas colored end-opening style case (by the fall of 1938 the cases were coming in black).

The "Lone Ranger" guitar was glossy black with a terrific scene painted in red and silver. The scene showed the Lone Ranger riding atop his horse Silver. Silver is reared up on hind legs. To the right of the scene is Tonto riding his horse Scout. Off in the distance is a steam engine train silhouetted against the full moon. The name "Lone Ranger" was stenciled in silver paint on the black peghead. The earliest "Lone Ranger" guitars didn't have any words painted on the body, but by the spring of 1937 the words "Hi-Yo Silver! The Lone Ranger" accompanied the scene. The spelling of "Hi-Yo Silver" changed in the fall of 1938 to "Hi-Ho Silver". Early "Lone Ranger" guitars had a fretboard painted in silver crystalline finish with black dots. In the fall of 1939 the fretboard changed to ebonized with speckled silver paint and four red position dots.

**Mid 1930's Supertone "Lone Ranger" predates the model with words painted on the scene, very rare.**

To give the look of binding, a red stripe was painted on the top edge of the body and encircled the soundhole. The 1936 through early 1938 models had wooden bridge pins with abalone inlays; afterwards, the bridge pins were made of celluloid. The last time the Lone Ranger model was advertised in the Sears catalog was the spring of 1941. The catalog described some interesting accessories that came with the guitar, which included the Long Ranger's 60 songs, enameled badge, pick, brightly colored neck cord and instruction book.

**Fall of 1937 "Lone Ranger" guitar, "Hi-Yo Silver!" black with scene painted in silver and red, Supertone Label, made by Harmony, sold through Sears.**

The Lone Ranger Rides Again, 1939

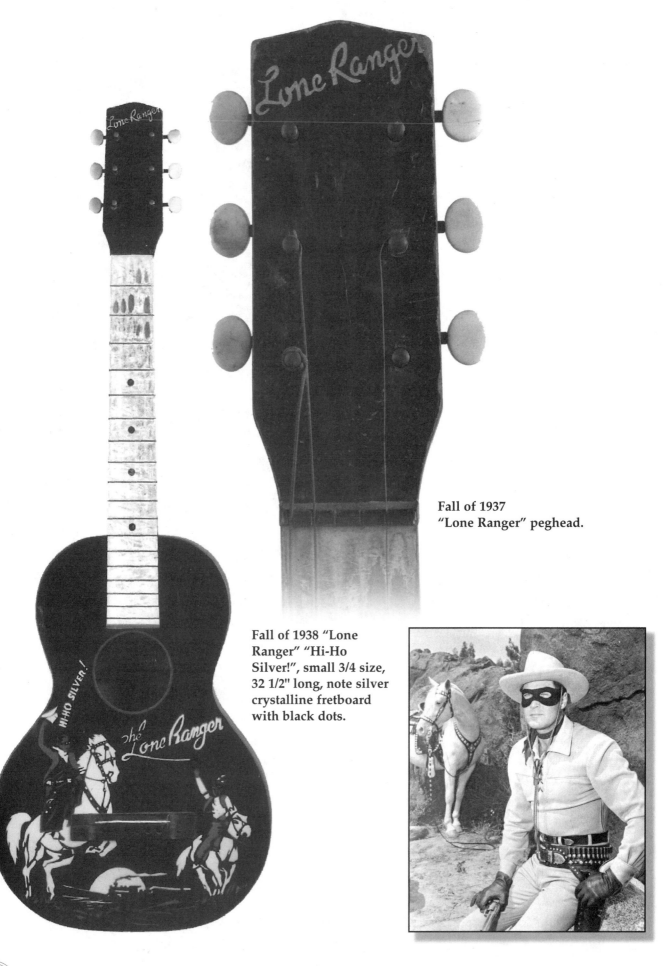

Fall of 1937
"Lone Ranger" peghead.

Fall of 1938 "Lone Ranger" "Hi-Ho Silver!", small 3/4 size, 32 1/2" long, note silver crystalline fretboard with black dots.

HI-HO SILVER!

The Lone Ranger

1939 "Lone Ranger" "Hi-Ho Silver!", standard size 36" long,
note silver splattered fretboard with red position dots.

# "LONE RANGER" GUITAR

## as Sold by
## T. Eaton Company (Made in Canada)

From 1937 through the spring of 1950, Eaton's offered a "Lone Ranger" guitar. The standard size (36 1/2" X 13 1/4") birch guitar was painted ebony black with the scene painted in red and silver. The scene was the same as on the "Lone Ranger" guitar sold by Sears & Roebuck. The 1937 model had a silver crystalline fretboard, an ebonized pin bridge and red striping painted around the soundhole and top edge just like the ones sold by Sears in the U.S. Some pre 1940 "Long Ranger" guitars sold by Eaton may have in fact been made by Harmony, but after 1940 they were made in Canada. A "Lone Ranger" with a "reversed" scene was shown in the 1938 catalog. This was either a mistake by the catalog's art department or a very unusual model. The words "Hi-Yo Silver, The Lone Ranger" were not in reverse, but the scene, which may have been painted using a stencil that had been flipped over on its other side, was a mirror image of the normal "Lone Ranger".

By the fall of 1941 the fretboard was coming ebonized (black) with three white position dots. The squared off slotted peghead had geared tuning keys with black buttons. The slotted peghead is one feature that distinguishes Eaton's Canadian "Lone Ranger" from the Sears "Lone Ranger" model, which had a solid peghead. From the fall of 1939 through the spring of 1946, Eaton's "Lone Ranger" guitar was advertised as available in both standard size and three-quarter size, but subsequent catalogs only mentioned the "Lone Ranger" as a standard size guitar. Eaton's 1943 spring catalog showed the "Lone Ranger" guitar with a few changes. Instead of a pin bridge, it had a black metal tailpiece with a moveable wooden bridge. And instead of geared tuners, it had "war era" wooden friction pegs. By the fall of 1947 geared tuning pegs were back in use, and at the same time the guitar was no longer coming with red striping painted around

the top edge of the body and soundhole. By the spring of 1948 the black metal tailpiece was coming 1/2" shorter in length, and in the fall of 1949 it was changed to shiny nickel-plated.

The wording on the body went through a few minor changes over the years. Starting with the 1938 model, the words read "Hi-Yo Silver, The Lone Ranger", but by the spring of 1943, the spelling of "Hi-Yo" had changed to "Hi-Ho", and in the spring of 1948 changed back to "Hi-Yo". There were no words painted on the slotted peghead.

**Pair of Canadian made "Lone Ranger" guitars, on the left is an early 1940's model with a pin bridge, on the right is a circa 1948 model with a gun-metal black trapeze tailpiece.**

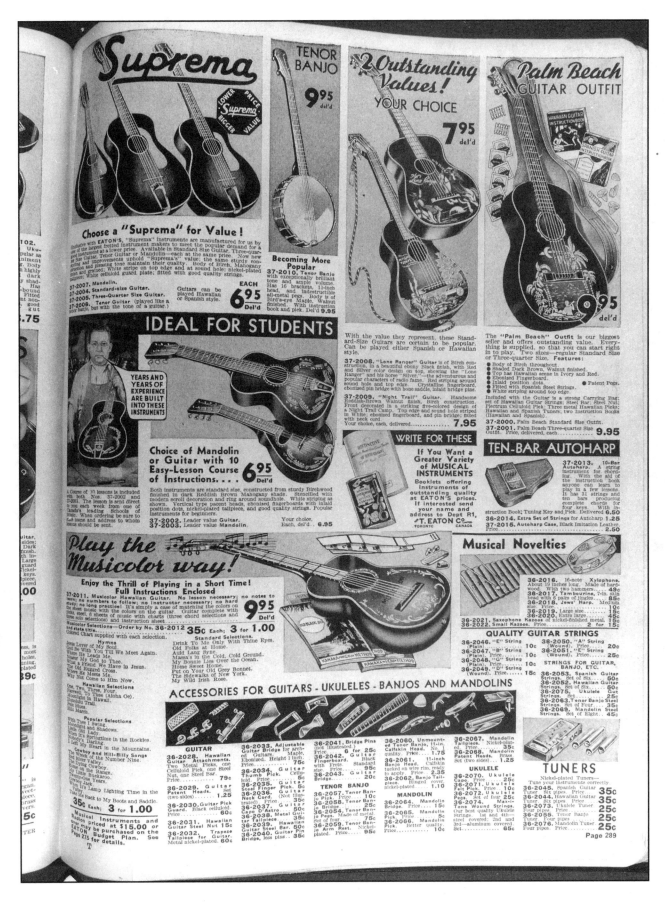

T. Eaton's 1938-1939 fall and winter catalog shows a couple of Canadian made cowboy guitars. The "Lone Ranger" shown here is very unusual because it has a reversed scene. Also shown is the "Night Trail" guitar.

Mid 1940's "Lone Ranger" made in Canada, war-era model with friction tuning pegs, all black with red and silver scene, with factory overspray from stencil painting, as sold through Eaton's.

Late 1940's "Lone Ranger", "Hi-Yo Silver!", made in Canada, standard size 36 1/2" long, shiny nickel-plated trapeze tailpiece with moveable wooden bridge, three position dots.

# "LONE RANGER" UKULELE
## as Sold by
## T. Eaton Company

In the fall of 1939 Eaton's offered a "Lone Ranger" ukulele. It was made of birch and was painted ebony black. The scene was painted in red and silver. The scene showed the Lone Ranger riding his horse Silver, and at the top of the scene were the words "Hi-Ho Silver".

# "LONE RANGER" GUITAR
## as Sold by
## Montgomery Ward

From the fall of 1950 through the spring of 1951, Ward's offered a "Lone Ranger" model guitar. This model was made for Ward's by the Harmony Company. The scene was the same as the late '30's Sears Lone Ranger, but the paint colors were different. The body, made of birch, had a walnut sunburst finish and the scene was painted in red and silver. A white stripe encircled the top and soundhole to give the look of binding. White triangular position markers were stencil-painted on the walnut color stained fretboard. Ward's referred to this guitar as standard size (35 3/4" X 13 1/4"). This guitar sported the easily identifiable Harmony nickel-plated trapeze tailpiece with heart and crescent cutouts.

Circa 1950-1951 "Lone Ranger", brown sunburst
with scene in red and silver, stencil-painted
triangular position markers, nickel-plated tailpiece
with heart and crescent shaped cutouts.

Mid 1960's "Lone Ranger" model guitar,
made by Jefferson, 29 3/4" fiberboard guitar,
orange to cream sunburst with scene in
white and black.

HI-YO SILVER!

*Jefferson's No. 85*
**"LONE RANGER"***
**COWBOY GUITAR**

All the romance and rhythm of
America's cowboy ballads come
to life on this fine guitar. Rich
professional tone, six strings,
standard tuning pegs. Lacquer-
sprayed finish; silk-screened
decorations. Comes with shoul-
der-cord and instructions for
tuning and playing. Children 6
and up. $3.98.†

**JEFFERSON MFG. CO.**
2433 N. Orianna St., Phila. 33, Pa.

1956 catalog advertisement
for Jefferson "Lone Ranger"
cowboy guitar.

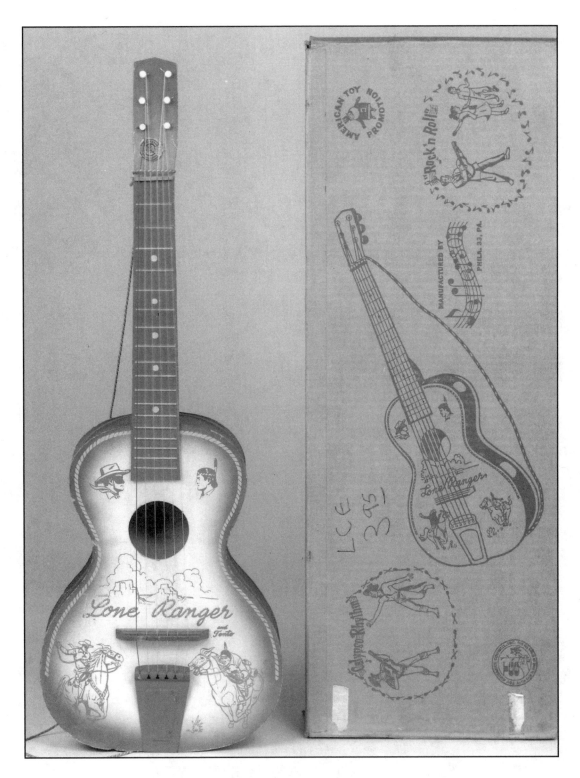

Late 1950's "Lone Ranger and Tonto", made by Jefferson, 30 1/2" fiberboard guitar, orange to cream sunburst with scene in green and yellow, shown here with original box.

Photography model, Monica Jean, is shown here with a circa 1955
Lone Ranger guitar made by Jefferson Manufacturing.

# THE LONE RANGER

*A fiery horse with the speed of light…a cloud of dust and hearty "Hi-yo, Silver." The Lone Ranger…*That opening became the standard introduction on radio and TV to a fictional character who is now part of the language of our times. The Lone Ranger rode for the first time January 30, 1933 over radio station WXYZ in Detroit, Michigan. The three-time-a-week series continued into the 1950s. The owner of the station, George W. Tredleand, tried original programming starting with a western. He envisioned its hero as being a dashing Douglas Fairbanks type. Someone suggested a mask, making the hero a western Robin Hood. He could even be a former Texas Ranger. "The lone ranger," someone else said. A legend was born and I won't repeat the origin of the character here, for it is an exciting story every fan knows. After a while people wanted to see as well as hear the Long Ranger, so Trendle offered movie rights. Republic got them, and promised to enhance the radio image.

*Say, Who Was That Masked Man?* The Lone Ranger was Clayton Moore. As he often said, "I was that Masked Man."

Moore was born September 14, 1914 in Chicago. He was a trapeze artist and male model before turning to acting. His face was familiar, mask or not, to anyone who saw many of the Republic and Columbia serials on the late 1940s. He was the "King of the Serials" at the time he was interviewed for the part. But once he became TVs Lone Ranger, his face was not seen unless he was wearing a disguise, where he admonished you to eat all your cereal, mind your folks, do your best at school, be kind to animals, practice safety and above all…be a good American.

*…With his faithful Indian companion, Tonto, the daring and resourceful masked rider of the plains, led the fight for law and order in the early western United States… Return with us now to those thrilling days of yester-year. From out of the past come the thundering hoofbeats of the great horse, Silver. The Lone Ranger rides again!*

Jay Silverheels, a full-blooded Mohawk Indian, was of course Tonto, born on the Six Nations Reservation in Brantford, Ontario, Canada. He had been a professional Lacrosse player and a champion middleweight boxer before turning to acting. Tonto played a Potawotamie Indian in the series, and with his paint horse Scout, doing 169 television episodes and two full-length motion pictures plus heavy touring. "Kimo Sabe?" why, everyone knows that means "Trusty Scout" or "Faithful Friend". Jay passed away March 5, 1980.

Moore said, "Wherever I go, in all my personal appearances, I always leave a silver bullet (aluminum) with *Lone Ranger 45* stamped on the cap. It's my trademark."

Moore broke into the national headlines again in 1979 when a California company that said it owned the rights to the Lone Ranger image went to court to stop Moore from making public appearances as the Lone Ranger. Moore appeared at dozens of "Save the Mask" rallies but a California judge unmasked Moore on September 3, 1979, for five years. Moore continued wearing the Lone Ranger outfit but with large dark sunglasses instead of the mask. Moore passed away December 28, 1999.

It's been said that a true intellectual is one who can listen to Rossini's William Tel Overture and not think of the Lone Ranger.

# "NIGHT TRAIL" GUITAR
## as Sold by
## T. Eaton Company

From the fall of 1938 through the summer of 1939, the "Night Trail" guitar was offered by Eaton's. The standard size (36 1/2" X 13 1/4") birch guitar was finished in a reddish brown walnut color with a multicolored scene painted in tan, rust, yellow, green, blue and silver. The scene showed three men gathered around a campfire where a stew pot was hanging. Smoke from the fire was shown streaming up the left side of the guitar to where the name "Night Trail" was painted. On the right side was a buckboard wagon and a big tree off in the distance. White striping was painted around the soundhole and the top edge of the body. The pin bridge and fretboard were ebonized and the neck had a squared off slotted peghead.

1940 "Trail Rangers", "Pastime" name painted on peghead, standard size, birch body.

1940 "Trail Rangers", dark natural walnut colored finish with multicolored scene, similar to Eaton's "Night Trail" scene, note tailpiece shown in this photo might be unoriginal, made by Harmony.

# "ROUND UP"/"RODEO"
## as Sold by
## Montgomery Ward

Wards introduced their "Round Up" model guitar in the spring of 1937. The name "Round-Up" was being used on a competitor's guitar (Sears' Gene Autry "Round-Up"), so by the fall of 1937 Wards had changed the name to "Rodeo".

Circa spring of 1937 "Round Up" sold through Wards.

# "Round Up"

The Wards "Round Up" was available in the spring of 1937. It had an action scene of three cowboys on horseback "whooping it up"; with the word "Round Up" painted above. The scene does look more like a rodeo than a round-up, one cowboy is shown riding and roping, another is waving his hat while riding a horse that is reared up on hind legs, and a third cowboy off in the distance is riding a bucking bronco. Also shown are a cactus, sagebrush, mountains and clouds. The scene painted in red and white, contrasts nicely against the all black guitar. The ebonized bridge had wooden bridge pins and a piece of fret wire for a saddle. The body was made of birch and measured 13 1/4" at the lower bout by 36 3/4" in total length. The neck had a slotted peghead with a wooden nut and an ebonized fretboard with fancy position markers painted in white. As with many guitars offered by Wards in the 1930's, a Hawaiian extension nut and steel bar would be included for an additional charge.

**Spring of 1937 "Round Up", "Round Up" name painted on upper left, black guitar with scene painted in red and white.**

I heard about a cowgirl out in Utah, nicknamed "Tad" who rode a horse from Canada 'cause he was big and bad. He knew a hundred wicked tricks and he would try them all, but Tad stayed in the saddle–she couldn't make her fall. Tad Lucas on "Juarez," Salt Lake City, Utah, 1924.

# "Rodeo"

From the fall of 1937 through the fall of 1938, Ward's offered the "Rodeo" guitar. The "Rodeo" had the same scene and specifications as the "Round-Up" except for the new name.

July 1938 "Rodeo", "Rodeo" name painted on upper left, pin bridge with fret wire saddle and wooden bridge pins, sold through Wards.

July 1938 "Rodeo", slotted peghead, "Flying Bats" position markers painted on ebonized fretboard.

# "HOME ON THE RANGE" GUITARS
## As Sold By
## Montgomery Ward

From 1938 through 1939, Wards offered the "Home on the Range" guitar. "The Home on the Range" model guitars were made for Wards by the Richter Company of Chicago. The spring 1938 model's scene looked like it had been done by an amateur artist. The new scene came out in the fall of 1938, which was much more attractive.

## "Old" Model

The "Home on the Range" was introduced by Wards in the spring of 1938. The poor artwork scene showed a cowboy playing guitar while sitting next to a hacienda. Also, a horse, cactus and mountains could be seen in the background. The words "Home on the Range" were painted at the top of the scene. The artwork and striping around the top edge and soundhole were painted in an ivory color. The body, made of birch, had a shaded walnut finish on front and back. The back of the neck had a very pronounced "V" shape and the rosewood colored fretboard had three inlaid position dot markers and brass frets. The ebonized bridge had wooden bridge pins and the saddle was a piece of brass fret wire. The Wards catalog for the spring of 1938 showed the guitar was available in standard size (36 3/4" X 13 1/4"), 3/4 size (33" X 11 1/4") and a tenor (four string) model that had a nickel-plated tailpiece.

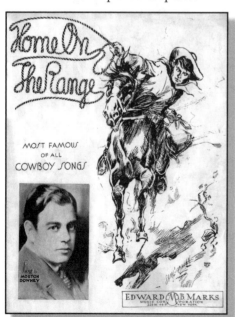

**Music sheet of
"Home On The Range" circa 1935**

**December 1937 "Home on the Range" poor artwork scene model, brown sunburst with scene painted in ivory color, standard size, 36 3/4 long, made by Richter, sold through Wards.**

# "New" Model

By July of 1938 the artwork of the scene had been changed to be more attractive. Wards offered the new scene model from the fall of 1938 through the spring of 1939. The new scene had the same theme, but now showed two cowboys and two horses. The coloring of the scene had been changed to black paint with white striping on the top edge and around the soundhole. The guitar specifications remained the same except for the bridge being a rosewood color instead of black. The guitar only came in the standard size (36 3/4" X 13 1/4"), the old model's 3/4 size and tenor guitar were no longer available. Wards' spring 1939 catalog showed that, for an extra charge, the guitar could be ordered with an extension nut and a steel bar for playing Hawaiian music.

**November 1938 "Home on the Range" birch body, made by Richter, sold through Wards.**

**November 1938 "Home on the Range" attractive scene model, brown sunburst with black scene and white striping, pin bridge with fret wire saddle and wooden bridge pins.**

# "SEVEN COWBOYS"
## Scene Guitar
## as Sold by Spiegel

From the spring of 1938 through the fall of 1952, intermittently, Spiegel offered a cowboy guitar with seven cowboys shown in the scene. This model was made by the Kay Musical Instrument Company for Spiegel. One of the catalogs described the guitar as having a roundup scene, but it looks more like some kind of cowboy meeting. A cowboy with a raised hand appears to be in discussion with a cowboy who is shown from the back. There are two cowboys on horses and three cowboys sitting cross-legged on the ground – one is holding a guitar. In the middle of the group of cowboys there is a campfire with smoke streaming up the length of the guitar body. At the lower left is a cactus and on the upper left the moon and clouds are shown.

Spiegel introduced the "Seven Cowboys" guitar in the spring of·1938. It had the Del Oro name painted on the peghead. The body was made of birch and it came in a walnut colored sunburst finish. It was available in standard size (36 1/4" X 13 1/2") with 12 frets clear of the body, and also in a large grand concert size (39" X 14 3/4"). It had a nickel-plated trapeze tailpiece with a moveable wooden bridge. The initials of the owner on three gold leaf pick-shaped decals came with the guitar at no extra charge. From the fall of 1938 through the fall of 1939, the "Seven Cowboys" scene was not available.

In the spring of 1940 catalog it was available again and only in the standard size; the grand concert size had been discontinued.

The "Seven Cowboys" was dropped from the line from the spring of 1941 through the spring of 1946. It was reintroduced in the fall of 1947 as an auditorium size (37 3/4" X 13 1/4") with fourteen frets clear of the body. At about the same time the brand name on the peghead had been changed from "Del Oro" to "Old Kraftsman". The three pick-shaped initials were no longer available to be ordered with the guitar. Another change for the 1947 model was a trapeze tailpiece with visible string slots as opposed to the old style trapeze with hidden string attachment; however, the old style trapeze would show up again in the 1949 fall catalog. Up through 1949 a Hawaiian conversion kit could be purchased with the "Seven Cowboys" guitar. The kit included an extension nut, steel bar, thumb and finger picks and a Hawaiian instruction book.

By the fall of 1950 a third type of tailpiece was in use. Instead of the traditional trapeze with an opening in the middle, the 1950 semi-trapeze tailpiece was solid with a raised area in the middle. The "Seven Cowboys" model guitar made its farewell appearance in Spiegel's 1952 fall catalog.

**These seven cowboys stopped just long enough to take out their guitars, tune up and sing to the other cowboys and put the horses to sleep. John Wayne, center, with no hat and playing that G chord, began and ended his singing career with this Republic Pictures movie "Westward Ho".**

Circa 1949 Old Kraftsman
cowboy guitar, auditorium
size, 37 3/4" long, 14 frets
clear of the body, made by
Kay, sold through Spiegel.

Circa 1949 Old Kraftsman, scene shows seven
cowboys, light brown sunburst birch guitar with
scene painted in white, old style trapeze tailpiece.

Circa late 1930's unusual model with "Seven Cowboys" scene, dobro style "f" holes, slotted peghead.

Circa late 1930's unusual model with "Seven Cowboys" scene, brown sunburst with scene painted in bright yellow, dobro style "f" holes, floral decorations on fretboard.

Entertainer Wylie Gustafson and his "Seven Cowboys" guitar, with sound hole pick up.
Photo: Bill Watts,
www.billwatts.com

# "PLAINSMAN" GUITAR
## as Sold by
## Montgomery Ward

From the fall of 1938 through the spring of 1943, Wards offered the "Plainsman" guitar. The "Plainsman" scene, painted in white and black, showed a cowboy on horseback standing beside a big pine tree. The guitar body was made of birch and was finished in enameled lacquer gunmetal gray. A white stripe was painted on the top edge of the body and around the soundhole. The strings attached to a nickel-plated trapeze tailpiece and crossed over an ebonized moveable bridge. The neck had a non-slot peghead that had the name "The Plainsman" painted in white. The ebonized fretboard had four inlaid position dots. The guitar came in standard size (36 1/2" X 14 1/2") or 3/4 size (31 3/4" X 11 1/2"). An optional extension nut and steel bar for Hawaiian style playing could be ordered with the "Plainsman".

### The Plainsman

No doubt the naming of this cowboy guitar was taken from this very popular movie.

A 1936 Paramount picture conceived and executed typical of a Cecil B. De Mille…epic, big budgets, big casts and big stories with an imaginary romance between Wild Bill Hickok and Calamity Jane. The cast included Gary Cooper as the austere Wild Bill Hickok, Jean Arthur as breezy Calamity Jane, and Charles Bickford as the smooth, gun running villain. All 64 pistols used in the film came from De Mille's personal collection.

**Late 1930's "Plainsman", resembles a scene right out of the 1936 Gary Cooper movie called "The Plainsman".**

**Late 1930's "Plainsman" guitar, standard size, 36 1/2" long, gunmetal gray finish with scene painted in black and white, sold through Wards.**

In late 1939 the color of the guitar was changed to a bronze colored lacquer finish with the scene painted in brown and white and the standard size measurement changed to 36 1/2" X 13 1/8".

November 1939 "Plainsman", standard size, 36 1/2" long, bronze colored finish with scene painted in brown and white, made by Richter

October 1939 "Plainsman", small 3/4 size 31 3/4" long, bronze colored finish with scene in brown and white, made by Richter for Wards.

In late 1940 the color of the guitar had changed back to gunmetal gray with the scene in white and black. At the same time the trapeze tailpiece changed to a new "lyre" shape with five vertical bars instead of two.

**Circa 1940 "Plainsman" in gunmetal gray, art work is painted in white and black, shows a cowboy on horseback standing beside a big pine tree, made by Richter for Wards. Also shown in this photo is a modern production cowboy gig bag.**

In the spring of 1941 the "Plainsman" could be ordered in gunmetal gray or blond (cream colored) with black and brown scene. By late 1941 the gunmetal gray color had been discontinued, but the blond finish was still available.

**Scenes from the film "The Plainsman."**

**Gary Cooper with Victor Varconi and Jean Arthur in a scene from "The Plainsman".**

**Charles Bickford and Gary Cooper in a scene from "The Plainsman".**

**1941 "Plainsman", standard size, 36 1/2" long, blond finish with scene in black and brown, made by Richter, note "Lyre" shaped tailpiece.**

In early 1942 there were no "Plainsman" guitars produced at all, but in the fall of 1942 a new and different "Plainsman" came out. The body was made of birch with a light brown sunburst top, and scene painted in ivory color. A white stripe was painted on the top edge and soundhole. Instead of the trapeze tailpiece, this model came with a wooden pin bridge. Because of World War II, the use of metal for luxury items was restricted, and the 1942 "Plainsman" had no metal parts. The neck had a slotted peghead with violin-style tuning pegs. The ebonized fretboard had three painted on green tree position markers and the very unusual feature of wooden maple frets. This model came in standard size (37" X 12 1/4") or 3/4 size (36" X 12"). By late 1943 the war was at full tilt and production of guitars had stopped.

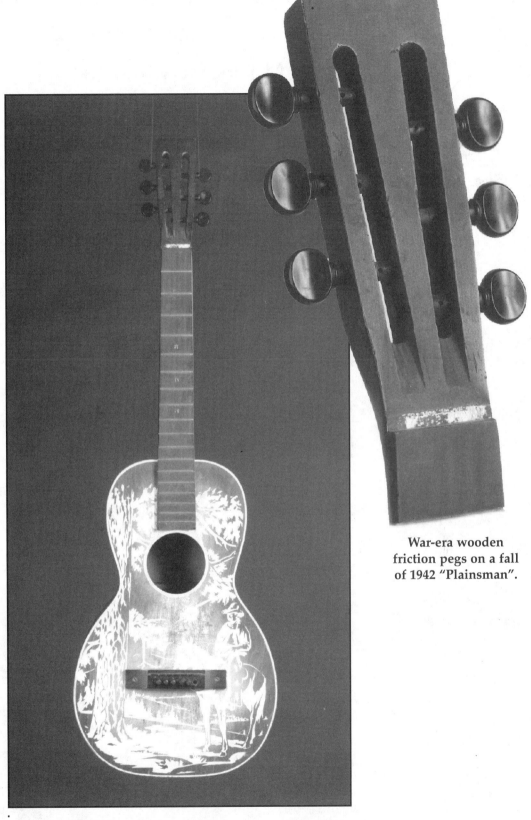

**War-era wooden friction pegs on a fall of 1942 "Plainsman".**

**Circa fall of 1942 "Plainsman", light brown sunburst with ivory colored scene, war-era model, no metal parts, wooden pin bridge, wooden frets, wooden friction pegs, this one made by Regal for Wards.**

# "PLAINSMAN" UKULELE

## as Sold by
## Montgomery Ward

From the fall of 1939 through the spring of 1940, Wards offered the "Plainsman" ukulele. The "Plainsman" uke had a birch body with a lacquered finish in a bronze color. The stenciled cowboy scene was painted in brown. The scene is a miniaturized version of the "Plainsman" guitar scene, showing a cowboy on horseback standing beside a big pine tree. A painted white stripe encircled the edge of the body and the soundhole, giving the look of binding. Wards referred to this uke as "standard size" (21" X 7").

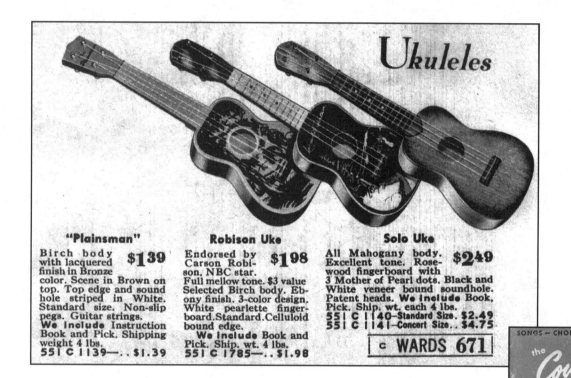

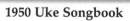

1950 Uke Songbook

**1936 Vaquero "Rodeo Scene"**

**Circa 1935 "Hill Billy Band"**

**1950's Rancher**

**Circa 1949 Old Kraftsman**

**Early '40's greenish-gray**

**Early '40's sunburst**

**1940's blond (cream)**

**1950's natural finish**

*"Jerry The Yodeling Cowboy"*

**1937 "Roundup"**

**1938 "Rodeo"**

**Early '40's gray "corral scene"**

**Early '40's red "corral scene"**

**Circa 1930 Bradley Kincaid**
**"Houn' Dog"**

**1943 "Singing Cowboys"**

**Mid '60's "Prairie Ramblers"**

**1964 "Trail Driver"**

1951 "Pioneer Days",
made in USA

Circa 1960 "Wagon Train",
made in Canada

Mid '50's "Roy Rogers",
made in USA

1958 "Roy Rogers",
made in Canada

"Texan", made in Holland

Circa 1943 "Powder River, Jack Lee"

1958 "Lariat"

1957 "King of the West"

1957 "Black Stallion"

1942 "Plainsman"

1950's Buckeye

Early '40's lefty cowboy scene

1937 "Home On The Range"

1938 "Home On The Range"

1935 "Wilf Carter"

Circa 1951 "Wilf Carter"

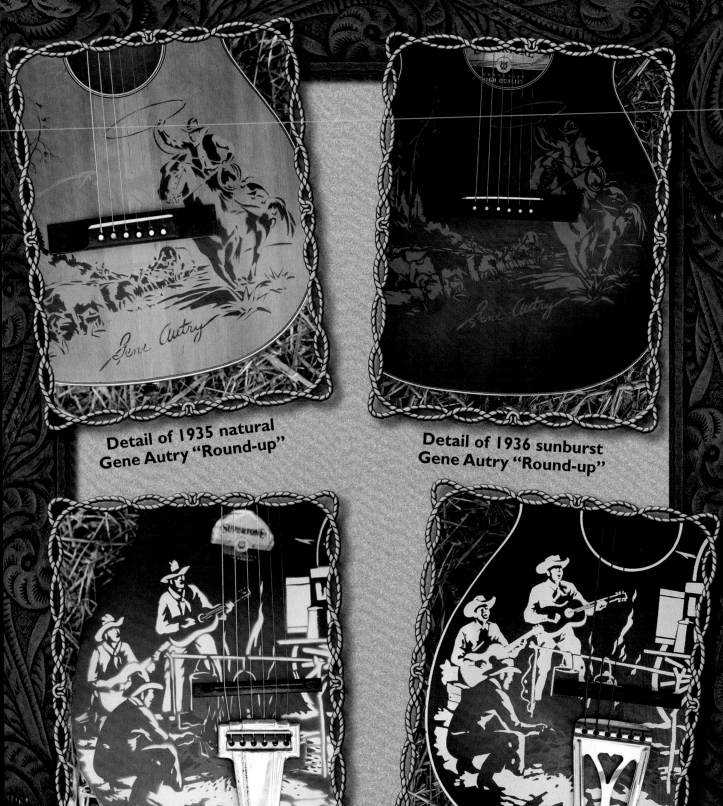

**Detail of 1935 natural
Gene Autry "Round-up"**

**Detail of 1936 sunburst
Gene Autry "Round-up"**

**Detail of circa 1940
"Singing Cowboys"**

**Detail of 1967
"Singing Cowboys"**

Circa '50's Rancher
"Pal O' Mine"

## "Ukuleles"

Late '30's
"Carson J. Robison"

Carnival brand
"Cowboy
Guitar" plastic
ukes in red swirl, yellow swirl and cream
colors, 15" long, with matching cowboy scenes.

1936-1937
style scene

Circa 1950 Kenny Roberts
"Little Pal"

**Circa early '60's
Range Rhythm "Wrangler"**

**1956 Jefferson "Texan Jr."**

**Circa 1957 Range Rhythm
"Roy Rogers"**

**Early '70's Jefferson "Roy Rogers"**

**Tin cowboy guitar**

**Late '50's "Cowboy Ge-tar"**

**1996 "Palomino Pony" and "Texan Jr."**

**1940 Richter cowboy guitar**

**1939-1941 Gene Autry "Round-up"**

**1959 Silvertone**

**Late '30's Plainsman**

**Standard size "Lariat" and
3/4 size "Western Rex"**

**Early '40's "Red Foley"**

**1937 "Lone Ranger"**

**1942 "Buck Jones"**

**Early '40's Gene Autry
"Melody Ranch"**

**1956 "Roy Rogers"**

**Father and Son Tele Set**
Fender Custom Shop
J. W. Black & John English

**La Riata**
Fender Custom Shop
Fred Stuart

**Western Set**
Fender Custom Shop
Alan Hamel

**Rodeo Girl**
Girl Brand Guitars
Chris Larsen

**First Martin Stencil Guitar**
C. F. Martin Custom Shop

**Cowboy X Limited Edition**
C. F. Martin

**Collings Guitars**

**Roy Rogers**
Greg Rich

# "SINGING COWBOYS" GUITAR

## as Sold by
## Sears, Roebuck & Co.

From Christmas of 1938 through the spring of 1943, Sears offered the "Singing Cowboys" model guitar. This model was made by the Harmony Musical Instrument Company for Sears. The "Singing Cowboys" scene shows five cowboys sitting around a campfire singing, two of them playing guitars. A chuck wagon with open cupboard doors appears to have different objects and containers within. On the ground is a trunk with one of the cowboys sitting on top holding a cup of coffee. A big coffeepot is hanging over the fire with two large stew pots nearby. The first issue (1938) did not have any words painted on the body, but in 1939 the words "Singing Cowboys" were added to the scene. On the guitar's upper bouts the words "Singing Cowboys" were painted in bright red, as was the campfire. The rest of the scene was painted in a cream color and gave the illusion of being illuminated by the campfire during the night.

Whoever designed the front of the "Singing Cowboy" guitar surly must have seen this old cowboy picture. Look how closely the chuck wagon matches, even the lamp on top and, of course, the artist used guitars instead of the banjo.

1938 "Singing Cowboys" guitar, note how this early model does not have the "Singing Cowboys" words painted on scene.

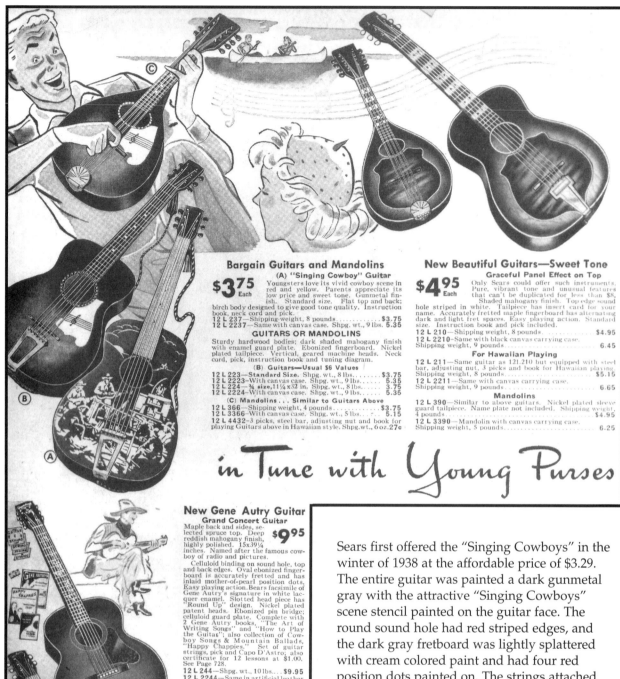

## Bargain Guitars and Mandolins

### (A) "Singing Cowboy" Guitar

**$3.75** Each

Youngsters love its vivid cowboy scene in red and yellow. Parents appreciate its low price and sweet tone. Gunmetal finish. Standard size. Flat top and back; birch body designed to give good tone quality. Instruction book, neck cord and pick.

12 L 237—Shipping-weight, 8 pounds............$3.75
12 L 2237—Same with canvas case. Shpg. wt., 9 lbs. 5.35

### GUITARS OR MANDOLINS

Sturdy hardwood bodies; dark shaded mahogany finish with enamel guard plate. Ebonized fingerboard. Nickel plated tailpiece. Vertical, geared machine heads. Neck cord, pick, instruction book and tuning diagram.

### (B) Guitars—Usual $6 Values

12 L 223—Standard Size. Shpg. wt., 8 lbs.......$3.75
12 L 2223—With canvas case. Shpg. wt., 9 lbs.... 5.35
12 L 224—¾ size,11¼ x52 in. Shpg. wt., 8 lbs. 3.75
12 L 2224—With canvas case. Shpg. wt., 9 lbs... 5.35

### (C) Mandolins . . . Similar to Guitars Above

12 L 366—Shipping weight, 4 pounds............$3.75
12 L 3366—With canvas case. Shpg. wt., 5 lbs... 5.15
12 L 4432—3 picks, steel bar, adjusting nut and book for playing Guitars above in Hawaiian style. Shpg.wt., 6 oz.27c

## New Beautiful Guitars—Sweet Tone

### Graceful Panel Effect on Top

**$4.95** Each

Only Sears could offer such instruments. Pure, vibrant tone and unusual features that can't be duplicated for less than $8. Shaded mahogany finish. Top edge sound hole striped in white. Tailpiece has insert card for your name. Accurately fretted maple fingerboard has alternating dark and light fret spaces. Easy playing action. Standard size. Instruction book and pick included.

12 L 210—Shipping weight, 8 pounds............$4.95
12 L 2210—Same with black canvas carrying case.
Shipping weight, 9 pounds...................... 6.45

### For Hawaiian Playing

12 L 211—Same guitar as 121.210 but equipped with steel bar, adjusting nut, 3 picks and book for Hawaiian playing. Shipping weight, 8 pounds..................$5.15
12 L 2211—Same with canvas carrying case.
Shipping weight, 9 pounds...................... 6.65

### Mandolins

12 L 390—Similar to above guitars. Nickel plated sleeve tailpiece. Name plate not included. Shipping weight, 4 pounds..................................$4.95
12 L 3390—Mandolin with canvas carrying case.
Shipping weight, 5 pounds...................... 6.25

## in Tune with Young Purses

## New Gene Autry Guitar

### Grand Concert Guitar

**$9.95**

Maple back and sides, selected spruce top. Deep reddish mahogany finish, highly polished. 15x39¼ inches. Named after the famous cowboy of radio and pictures.

Celluloid binding on sound hole, top and back edges. Oval ebonized fingerboard is accurately fretted and has inlaid mother-of-pearl position dots. Easy playing action. Bears facsimile of Gene Autry's signature in white lacquer enamel. Slotted head piece has "Round Up" design. Nickel plated patent heads. Ebonized pin bridge; celluloid guard plate. Complete with 2 Gene Autry books, "The Art of Writing Songs" and "How to Play the Guitar"; also collection of Cowboy Songs & Mountain Ballads, "Happy Chappies." Set of guitar strings, pick and Capo D'Astro; also certificate for 12 lessons at $1.00. See Page 728.

12 L 244—Shpg. wt., 10 lbs....$9.95
12 L 2244—Same in artificial leather side opening case. Shipping weight, 12 pounds...................$12.65

### Lone Ranger Guitar

Copyright 1938, The Lone Ranger, Inc.

#### Exclusive with Sears

**$5.75**

The "Lone Ranger" with its 'he-man' figure of radio's most beloved character, is the most popular guitar in America today. Buy it now at Sears usual savings.

Standard size. Hardwood body scientifically designed to give good tone. Ebony black finish with decorations in silver effect and red. Fingerboard in silver crystalline color finish. Vertical type machine heads. Stationary bridge with bone saddle and bridge pins with celluloid heads. Neck cord. Instruction book and pick included. See Page 728.

12 L 206—Shpg. wt., 8 lbs...$5.75
12 L 2206—With black canvas case. Shipping weight, 9 lbs........$7.25

#### Three-Quarter Size

For women, children and others with small hands. Shipping weight, 6 lbs.
12 L 207.....................$5.75
12 L 2207—With black canvas case. Shipping weight, 7 lbs........$7.25

PAGE 722 △ SEARS

Sears first offered the "Singing Cowboys" in the winter of 1938 at the affordable price of $3.29. The entire guitar was painted a dark gunmetal gray with the attractive "Singing Cowboys" scene stencil painted on the guitar face. The round sound hole had red striped edges, and the dark gray fretboard was lightly splattered with cream colored paint and had four red position dots painted on. The strings attached to a nickel-plated trapeze style tailpiece, and the moveable bridge was made of wood, as was the string nut. The tuning machines were simple three-on-a-side plank style with black buttons. The sturdy guitar body was made of birch. Referred to as "standard size", the guitar measured 13 1/8" wide at the lower bout by 35 3/4" in total length.

**Several cowboy guitars were shown in the spring of 1939 Sears catalog.**

By the fall of 1939 the tailpiece had been changed to an "Idento" made by Kluson. The "Idento" was a nickel-plated tailpiece with a place to insert an identification card, bearing the owner's name and concealing the string attachment.

Round blue & silver Supertone label inside soundhole of a circa 1940 "Singing Cowboys", made by Harmony, sold through Sears.

Circa 1940 "Singing Cowboys" gunmetal gray with scene in red and cream color, standard size, 35 3/4" long, dark gray fretboard with splattered cream colored paint, position dots painted in red, "idento" tailpiece.

In the fall of 1941 a 3/4 size became available. It measured 11 1/4" wide by 32 1/4" in total length. The early "Singing Cowboys" 3/4 size had an "Idento" tailpiece, but was changed in the fall of 1942 to have a glued on wooden pin bridge with no tailpiece. It had the same "Singing Cowboys" scene, but part of the stencil had been cut away to fit the smaller body. Instead of five cowboys shown, there were only three, though the scene is still attractive this way. The 3/4 size cost the same as the standard size (1941 price, $3.79). The 3/4 size was offered from the fall of 1941 until the spring of 1943. During the fall of 1941 and the spring of 1942, Sears offered personalized initials for application to the front of their guitars. By the spring of 1943 the guitar's finish had changed to black instead of gunmetal gray.

**Spring of 1942 "Singing Cowboys", small 3/4 size, 32 1/4" long, short version of "idento" tailpiece.**

**1943 "Singing Cowboys" model, black with chuck wagon scene in cream and red, note war-era wooden tailpiece.**

By the spring of 1943, with the war effort starting up, the metal tailpiece was dropped and a stationary ebonized tailpiece with a moveable wood bridge was used on the standard size (the 3/4 size had been switched to an all wood bridge six months earlier). By the fall of 1943 Sears had discontinued the "Singing Cowboys". Production of guitars in general came to a standstill during World War II.

Standard size and 3/4 size "Singing Cowboys" guitars, both made in the fall of 1942. Notice how part of the scene was not used on the smaller guitar and note the war era wooden tailpiece on the larger guitar. Holding the pair of 55-year-old guitars are Sarah Evans, 11 years old and Jenna Evans, 8 years old.

From 1951 through 1963 the Harmony Company catalogs showed a "Singing Cowboys" model with the name "Harmony" on the peghead. Its designated model number was 1057 and the retail price in 1951 was $19.50. It was painted with the same chuck wagon scene like the "Singing Cowboys" model offered by Sears. The scene was painted in cream with the "Singing Cowboys" lettering and the campfire in bright red. A white stripe painted around the top edge and soundhole gave the look of binding. Three sandwiched horizontal bars were painted in white at the 5th, 7th and 9th fret positions, a common appointment on many other Harmony models, as was the metal tailpiece with heart-and-crescent shaped cutouts. The moveable bridge and the nut were both made of wood.

**Spring of 1958 date stamp inside a Harmony "Singing Cowboys" model guitar.**

**Spring of 1958 Harmony "Singing Cowboys" brown sunburst with scene in cream and red, standard size, 35 5/8" long, note Harmony triple-bar sandwich position markers painted on fretboard and tailpiece with heart and crescent shaped cutouts.**

Advertised as "standard size", this guitar measured 13 1/4" wide at the lower bout by 35 5/8" in total length. The body was made of birch and had a shaded brown mahogany stained (sunburst) finish on front and back and on the back of the neck. The tuning keys were three-on-a-side plank style with plastic buttons.

**Close-up of peghead of spring of 1958 Harmony "Singing Cowboys".**

**1960's "Singing Cowboys", later style scene, made by Harmony in Chicago, Illinois, note "Steel Reinforced Neck" painted on peghead.**

By late 1963 the "Singing Cowboys" was no longer advertised in the Harmony catalog, but in the mid 1960's there was a "Singing Cowboys" produced with an updated scene. Its new model designation was number 929. The color of the chuck wagon scene had been changed from cream paint to white, giving a crisper look. The artwork was slightly different with subtle changes in the scene. The new model showed the cowboys wearing later date cowboy hats instead of the rounded "Hop-a-Long Cassidy" style hats, and the boots had been changed to be more pointed. The wagon looked more updated with the addition of drawers to the storage shelves. Even the two guitars in the scene looked a bit more modern compared to the slope-shoulder-shaped guitars in the old scene.

Singing cowboys at Home Ranch, by Thomas Eakins, 1888.

Fall of 1967 Harmony "Singing Cowboys"; later style chuck wagon scene showing cowboys wearing modern hats and pointy boots, sunburst with scene in white and red.

# HARMONY DATE STAMPS

The Harmony Company usually rubber stamped the season (S=Spring or F=Fall) and the year of manufacture inside their guitars. Red or blue ink was used in the 1930's and blue or black ink was used from 1940 on. Often the date may not be legible. However, the style of stamp can aid in dating the guitar. See the following info.

**S 35**　　Date in oval (F32 through S40)

**F-35**　　Date in rectangle (F-35 through S-39)
　　　　　This seldom used date stamp can be found in "Old Santa Fe"
　　　　　and grand concert "Round-Up", Gene Autry guitars.

**S42**　　Date, not in an oval or rectangle (S42 through F48)

　　　　Double box, date in small section (S49)

　　　　Triple box, date in right-hand small box (F50 through S51)

**F-55-T**　　Single box (F-51 through F-57)

**S-58-T GG**　　Double box, date in large section (F-57 through S-59)

**FL-59 WN**　　Date and USA info, not in a box (FL-59 through F-73)

# HARMONY "H" NUMBER

An eight or nine digit "H" number (rubber stamped in the area of neck block), was applied on Harmony guitars from 1942 through the early 1970's. This number was actually stamped twice inside the guitar; just in front of the neck block, as seen through the sound hole, and adjacent to this location, hidden from view on the underside of the top.

The "H" number doesn't help much in dating the guitar, but does give proof the guitar was made by Harmony. The "H" number consisted of three or four numbers, an "H" and three or four more numbers. The following examples show what they signify:

example **4501H610**

4501 = factory order number
"H" = Harmony
610 = model (Gene Autry, Melody Ranch)

There were some Harmony made guitars circa 1939 with the "H" number scheme, but instead had a different letter in the middle of the number.

example **3433E4250**

3433 = factory order number
"E" = T. Eaton Co. of Canada
4250 = model (Lone Ranger)

example **3249SR237**

3249 = factory order number
"SR" = Sears, Roebuck & Co.
237 = model (Singing Cowboys)

**Cowboy guitar side mold from the Chicago Harmony Guitar Co. made of aluminum. The wood was pre-soaked and bent around the mold and clamped at both ends. To increase the top weight, the round steel cylinder was added on top. The wooden handle was to lift the top part on and off the mold. The gas inlet to heat the mold was attached on top. It took about 20-25 minutes to mold each side. John Quarterman.**

# "SINGING COWBOYS" GUITAR

## as Sold by

## T. Eaton Company (Made in Canada)

During early 1941 and again in the summer of 1949, Eaton offered a "Singing Cowboys" guitar. The standard size (36 1/2" X 13 1/4") birch guitar was finished in jet black with the scene painted in red and ivory. The guitar's chuck wagon scene was a reproduction of the scene used on the "Singing Cowboys" model made by Harmony Company in Chicago. A couple of things that make the Canadian version look different from the US model are that the Canadian has a slotted peghead and that the tailpiece was a true trapeze shape with two separate points of attachment at the end of the body. When the "Singing Cowboys" model appeared again in the summer of 1949, the tailpiece had been changed to the trapeze style with a single point of attachment as found on the more modern Canadian made cowboy guitars.

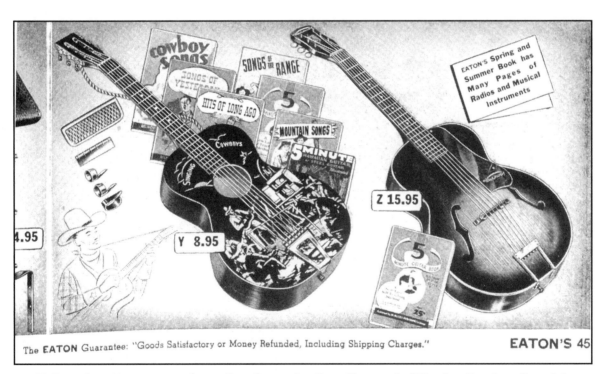

T. Eaton's 1949 summer sale catalog shows the Canadian-made "Singing Cowboys" model.

# "RAY WHITLEY" MODEL GUITARS
## as Sold
## by Montgomery Ward

From the spring of 1939 through the spring of 1940, Wards offered guitars endorsed by Ray Whitley. The two Ray Whitley models were both high quality guitars made by the Gibson Guitar Company for Wards. But instead of the Gibson brand, they sported the "Recording King" brand name. Both models had a steel rod in the neck, but had no visible truss rod adjustment.

The spring of 1939 is when the Ray Whitley "Recording King" was introduced. It was a jumbo size (41" X 16") flat-top guitar with a sunburst spruce top and natural finished Brazilian rosewood back and sides. This model compared to the Advanced Jumbo model in the Gibson line. The guitar top, back and fretboard had white celluloid binding. The fretboard was made of rosewood and had fancy diamond shaped mother-of-pearl inlays. The "Bat Wing" shaped rosewood pin bridge had three inlaid mother-of-pearl dots, which hid the screws securing the bridge to the top. The tortoise-shell celluloid pickguard had decorative engraving and was an unusual shape. The peghead had an inlaid mother-of-pearl small crown, the "Recording King" name painted in black over a mother-of-pearl rectangle shaped inlay, and a reproduction of Ray Whitley's signature stenciled in white.

In the fall of 1939 there were two Ray Whitley endorsed guitars. The new addition was basically the same as the rosewood back model, but had mahogany back and sides. Other differences were fretboard dot markers and a rectangular pin bridge with two inlaid mother-of-pearl dots. This model did not necessarily have the Ray Whitley signature on the peghead. When compared to the Gibson line, the mahogany back Ray Whitley model would be like a combination of a J-35 and a J-55.

The rosewood back model was available from the spring of 1939 through the fall of 1939. The mahogany back model was available from the fall of 1939 through the spring of 1940.

**Top right, Model similar to Brazillion Rosewood SJ
Bottom, Regular Jumbo, cross between a J35 and J55.**

# RAYMOND OTIS "RAY" WHITLEY

Despite a late start, Ray Whitley became a quite successful jack-of-all-trades in the era of the singing cowboy. He was born on December 5, 1901, near Atlanta, Georgia. He spent some time in the Navy and in Philadelphia.

Ray Whitley was an electrician and steel worker living in New York City where he pursued music as a hobby. There he was influenced by the success of Jimmie Rodgers. In 1931, he auditioned for WMCA Radio and was hired for a *Crazy Water Crystals* show as "Ray Whitley and his Range Ramblers." The following year he changed his band name to the Bar-Six Cowboys.

Whitley's recording career started in New York City with the Frank Luther Trio. In 1935, he was featured on the "WHN Barn Dance" with Tex Ritter. By 1936, Whitley moved to Dallas and from there traveled to Hollywood with a contract to appear in a Hopalong Cassidy movie. One of the earliest singing cowboys to invade Hollywood, he appeared in films as early as 1936. He spent 1938 to 1942 at RKO studios where he made 18 musical shorts of his own and was the singing sidekick to George O'Brien and Tim Holt. His last role was as Watts, James Dean's manager in the movie *Giant*.

Whitley collaborated with Gene Autry in writing *Back in the Saddle* (recorded by Autry in 1939). In the early 1940's, while working on the "Saddle Mountain Roundup," at KVOO Radio in Tulsa, he met Fred Rose. They co-wrote a few songs such as *Hang My Head and Cry* and *Lonely River*. His biggest hits were his theme song, *Blue Yodel Blues*, and *The Last Flight Of Wiley Post*. In addition to writing songs, Whitley had his own western-swing band in the 1940's, managed Jimmy Wakely and the Sons of the Pioneers. He also recorded western songs for Decca, Okeh and other labels.

One of Whitley's greatest contributions to western music was in 1937, when he helped Gibson Guitar Company design and build the singing cowboy's favorite guitar, the Gibson SJ-200.

He was still turning up at western film festivals, singing and doing tricks with his bullwhip until shortly before his death in California on February 21, 1979.

**Ray Whitley with the Phelps Brothers in back and Ken Card on banjo.**

# THE "BUCK JONES" GUITAR

## as Sold by
## Montgomery Ward

From the fall of 1940 through the spring of 1943, Wards offered a "Buck Jones" model guitar. This model was made by Regal for Wards. It had a detailed scene showing Buck Jones on his horse Silver, with an inscription reading "Good Luck, Buck Jones & Silver". Along with a big cactus and great billowy clouds of a prairie scene, this is one of the most attractive cowboy guitars. The scene was painted in black and white on the light brown sunburst guitar. The top was made of spruce, and the back and sides were maple (sometimes birds eye maple). The top edge and sound hole had white celluloid binding. The strings attached to a nickel-plated lyre-shaped tailpiece and crossed over a moveable ebonized wooden bridge. The neck had a bone nut and an ebonized fretboard with four inlaid mother-of-pearl position dots. On the back of the peghead, a nickel-plated canister covered the three tuning gears on each side.

The "Buck Jones" guitar came in standard size (37" X 13") and in a 3/4 size (36" X 12") and was available with an optional extension nut and slide bar for playing Hawaiian style.

"Buck Jones" guitars made by Regal circa 1940-41, the one on the left has wider upper bouts.

This publicity shot of Buck and Silver was used for the front of the guitar.

1933
Movie poster

This photo, taken in 1941, shows the Hall brothers on their farm in Guy, Arkansas. Notice fourteen-year-old J.D. Hall with his "new" Buck Jones guitar. J.D. says he ordered the guitar from Montgomery Wards for $4.98, money he had earned by chopping wood.

1930 Lobby card

1940's "Buck Jones" model guitar, made in Canada, natural finish with scene painted in black and white.

Spring of 1942 "Buck Jones" guitar, light brown sunburst with scene in black and white, real binding, lyre shaped tailpiece.

By the spring of 1942 the Kluson brand tuning keys were no longer coming with canisters covering the gears, and the white key buttons were coming in black. At the same time the inlaid fretboard dots were smaller in size.

Circa 1941 "Buck Jones" model, made by Regal, sold through Wards, on back of the peghead are two metal canisters covering the tuning machines.

1951 April-June comic book

**Early 1940's "Buck Jones" guitar.**

In the fall of 1942 the "Buck Jones" had many changes. It was only available in standard size; the 3/4 size had been dropped. The finish had changed to a shiny lacquer finish. The top edge of the body had white painted-on striping instead of binding, although the sound hole (which was a little smaller in diameter) still had real binding. A wooden pin bridge with wooden bridge pins had replaced the metal tailpiece because of conservation of metal for the war effort. Toward the end of production the "Buck Jones" had changed to an all birch body. By mid 1943, production of the "Buck Jones" guitar had ceased because of World War II.

**Late 1940's Regal, natural finish, unusual "Buck Jones" scene with no signature. Bill Dye's parents purchased this guitar for him as a Christmas gift in 1947 at the U.S. Steel company store in Lynch, Kentucky. Even though it had high action, this guitar inspired Bill and his brothers, Larry and Gary to play guitar.**

**Fall of 1942 "Buck Jones" shiny lacquer finish, white striping instead of binding, wooden pin bridge.**

**Buck Jones**

# BUCK JONES

In the 1920s Buck Jones was one of the "big guns" at the Saturday matinees. Charles Frederick Gebhart, Charles "Buck" Jones and finally Buck Jones, was born December 12, 1891 in Vincennes, Indiana. His parents divorced when Buck was young. He and his sister Ada moved to Indianapolis and grew up there. He went as far as the 8th grade. In 1907, at age 16, he enlisted in the army when his mother signed a consent form saying he was 18. He was discharged December 20, 1909. After a short stay in Indianapolis, he re-joined the army on October 14, 1910. He gave his age as 21 and listed his occupation as "musician". He was discharged October, 1913 in Texas City, Texas.

He joined the famous Miller Brothers 101 Wild West Show. He didn't know much about being a cowboy but he knew horses and could ride well. Eventually he became an arena performer. While in New York, a beautiful equestrienne named Odille (Dell) Osborn joined the show. In 1915 she left the 101 show to go with the Julia Allen Wild West Show and Buck followed her. They got married during an actual performance.

Buck and Dell formed their own family riding expedition circus and toured the west where they joined the Ringling Brothers Circus. When they played Los Angeles, Dell was pregnant. Buck decided to quit Ringling and try to find a job with the studios. He was hired as a bit player and stunt man. Studio head William Fox decided he needed a back-up in case he lost Tom Mix. Fox took notice of Buck and in 1920 his first starring film, *The Last Straw* was released. Audiences responded and Charles Buck Jones became a star. Buck made at least 60 silent films for Fox. The silent era was ending and 'talkies' were arriving. Jones personally financed *The Big Hop*. It flopped. He then put together his "Buck Jones Wild West Show and Roundup Days." After a couple months, the show went bust. Buck went to work as the main attraction with the Robbins Brothers Circus for the 1929 season. He was off the screen for well over a year.

In 1930, connecting with Columbia Pictures, Jones' first talkie was "The Lone Rider". It was released through Columbia, but with the Beverly Productions company. The movies proved that Jones could handle dialog in a reasonably believable manner. Jones went to Universal and through 1937 did twenty-two films and three serials. Buck returned to Columbia, but the singin' cowboy had arrived. Buck no longer "fit in".

Buck tried his hand at a short-lived western radio serial in 1937-1938. From 1938-1940, film roles were few and far between. In 1941, he was in a new western trio series called *The Rough Riders*.

Jones died from injuries received in the November 28, 1942 Coconut Grove nightclub fire in Boston, which killed nearly 500 people. He passed away on November 30, 1942 at the Massachusetts General Hospital.

# "JERRY SMITH, THE YODELING COWBOY"

Circa early 1940's Regal "Jerry the Yodeling Cowboy", greenish-gray with scene painted in brown, has a square neck for playing Hawaiian style, note painted numbers on fretboard.

Early 1940's Regal "Jerry the Yodeling Cowboy" slotted peghead, dark green label with crown and "Regal" name in gold.

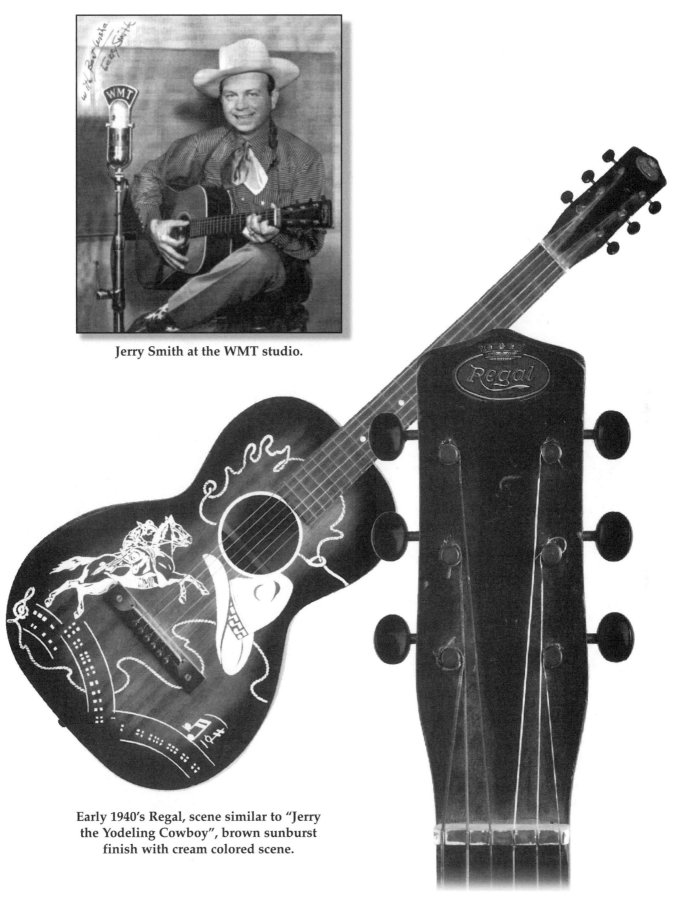

Jerry Smith at the WMT studio.

Early 1940's Regal, scene similar to "Jerry the Yodeling Cowboy", brown sunburst finish with cream colored scene.

Early 1940's Regal solid peghead with dark green "Regal" label.

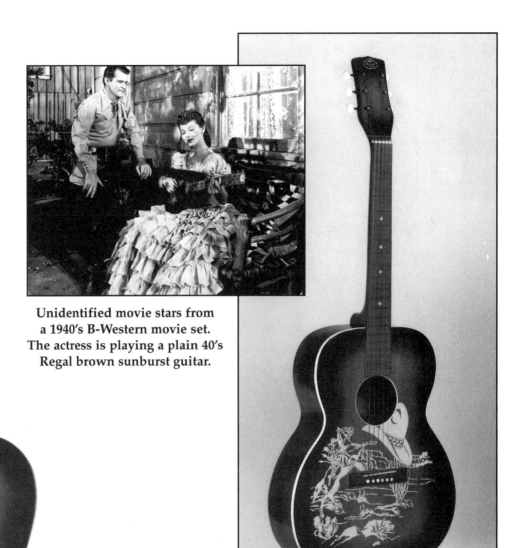

Unidentified movie stars from
a 1940's B-Western movie set.
The actress is playing a plain 40's
Regal brown sunburst guitar.

Large auditorium size (40 1/2" x 15 1/2")
Regal. Artwork consists of a cowboy on
reared horse, large "Hoppy" style hat, and
a prairie scene (desert scene?). The art
looks nice, painted in cream color on the
light brown sunburst guitar. The Regal
crown logo is stencil painted in white on
the peghead, instead of the typical decal.

**1940's Regal in orangish
brown to black sunburst.**

The Regal Musical Instrument Company was established in 1908. From
1930 to the 1950's they were one of the largest manufactures of musical
instruments. The Regal Company made their first concert guitar in 1927. In
1937 they had exclusive rights to manufacture and sell the Dobro resonator
guitars. In 1938 they started a direct-to-dealer policy, and in 1940 they
marketed a make-it-yourself kit for ukuleles.

The Regal Company built guitars for many other distributors under
several different brand names. The quality varied widely from the student-
grade to the very ornate.

Regal discontinued business in 1954, selling the name to the Harmony
Company. In 1959 Harmony built Regal brand acoustic guitars for Fender
until 1966.

1940's Regal peghead, light blue label with
crown in red and yellow,
and "Regal" name in yellow.

1940's Regal, with big rounded hat, sometimes referred to as a
"Hopalong Cassidy" scene, but is a combination of "Jerry the Yodeling Cowboy"
and the background from a "Buck Jones" scene. Cream colored guitar with
brown scene and black striping on top edge, note Kluson "idento" tailpiece.

Circa 1954 Regal, scene similar to "Jerry the Yodeling Cowboy", natural finish with black scene.

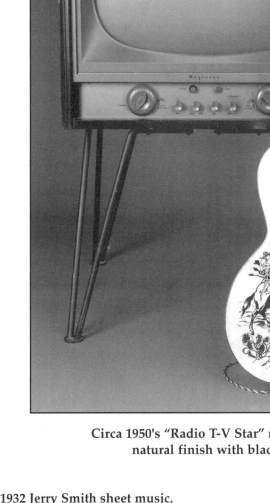

Circa 1950's "Radio T-V Star" made by Regal, natural finish with black scene.

1932 Jerry Smith sheet music, "Under the Old Apple Tree."

# JERRY SMITH

Jerry Smith was a range-riding cowboy who set out to be a veterinarian and ended up before the microphone, singing the songs of the cattlemen. He was known to millions of listeners as the "Yodeling Cowboy".

Jerry was born July 15, 1911. It was because of a love for horses that he enrolled in college with the intent upon becoming a veterinarian. After Jerry enrolled in the veterinarian school, he was struck with wanderlust, left school and set out to see the world. He finally wound up in the audition rooms of WWAE, Hammond, Indiana and was given his first radio job delighting radio listeners with his songs. From there he went to WJKS, Gary, Indiana and several other stations around

the country ending up in De Moines, Iowa at the radio station WHO, where he was very popular and found a long lasting home. He was named the Champion Yodeler of Iowa in a Statewide contest in 1938, recorded for Cattle, Cedar and Mastertone Records, and had several music folios.

Smith did leave Iowa long enough in 1940 to make one of the Range Busters' B Westerns for Monogram Studios, *West of Pinto Basin*. He was offered a contract to stay in Hollywood and continue his work in Western films but he declined. Iowa was where he wanted to be. Jerry was a regional superstar in the Midwest, enjoying a long career at WHO with a syndicated radio show.

**November 1939 publicity shot with his namesake guitar for radio station WHO Des Moines, Iowa. Photo courtesy Robert J. Sime**

1939

1941

# "LOUISE MASSEY" MODEL GUITAR

## as Sold by
## Montgomery Ward

Wards only offered the Louise Massey guitar in the fall of 1941. The Louise Massey model was made for Ward's by the Kay Musical Instrument Company of Chicago. It was an auditorium size (40 1/2" X 15") guitar finished in natural blond. The top was made of spruce and the back and sides were maple. A reproduction of Louise Massey's signature was painted in brown just below the bridge. The sculptured rosewood bridge had a bone saddle and white celluloid pins. The elongated tortoise colored pickguard was slightly elevated from the guitar top by small rubber grommets. The top edge, soundhole and fretboard had brown celluloid binding. The fretboard was made of rosewood and had four mother-of-pearl position dots. The peghead was painted brown and matched the color of the L. Massey signature and the guitar binding. The plank style tuning machines were covered with a canister on each side and had white tuning buttons.

Wards included with the guitar, a pick, neck cord, Spanish guitar instruction book, and a "Louise Massey and the Westerners" song folio – all for the reasonable price of $8.95.

"THE WESTERNERS"
(Massey Family)

**1941 "Louise Massey" model guitar, natural finish spruce top with maple back and sides, reproduction of Louise Massey signature painted in brown, auditorium size, 40 1/2" long, made by Kay, sold through Wards.**

# LOUISE MASSEY AND THE WESTERNERS

The Westerners, one of the most popular western bands in the thirties and forties, was a family band. Henry "Dad" Massey was the father of eight children, three of whom became professional musicians through his encouragement: Curt, Allen and Louise. These three were born in Midland, Texas, before their father decided to buy the K Bar Ranch near Roswell, New Mexico. Curt, the oldest son, was taught to play the violin by his father. Dad Massey taught his other children to play a variety of instruments.

In the 1920's the three children and their father were offered a contract to travel the Chatauqua circuit in the Midwest as the Massey Family Band which they did for two years. While in Kansas City, they were given radio time and stayed there for a few years. Dad Massey went back to the ranch in New Mexico, and Larry Wellington took his place. Louise married a New Mexico musician, Milt Mabie, who became a member of the band.

After a few years in Kansas City, they joined the WLS "National Barn Dance" in 1928. From there they went to New York City and were featured on the radio show "Showboat". When that show moved to Hollywood, they stayed in New York with their own radio show, "The Log Cabin Dude Ranch". Their popularity took them across the nation on personal appearance tours before returning to Chicago, WLS and the Plantation Party show. They were the first to dress in flashy cowboy outfits and exploit a western image.

They were first known as the *Musical Massey Family*. They changed from the family name to *The Westerners* and with Louise becoming more and more popular as the vocalist, they changed their name again to *Louise Massey and the Westerners*. They recorded for a variety of labels, Vocalion, Okeh, and Conqueror. Their biggest hit was probably *The Honey Song*, and Louise is best remembered for co-writing *My Adobe Hacienda*.

Band members were Milt Mabie (Louise's husband) - vocals and various instruments; Allen Massey - vocals and various instruments; Curt Massey - fiddle, trumpet, piano, vocals; Dad Massey - vocals and fiddle; Louise Massey - vocals; Larry Wellington - vocals and various instruments.

After disbanding, Curt continued his career in popular music and became the musical director and theme songwriter for the television shows *Beverly Hillbillies* and *Petticoat Junction*.

**1942 Sheet music**

# "RED FOLEY" SIGNATURE CONCERT SIZE GUITAR

## as Sold by
## Montgomery Ward

From the spring of 1942 through the spring of 1943, Ward's offered the "Red Foley" guitar. The "Red Foley" was made by Harmony for Wards. This concert size (37 3/4" X 14") guitar was finished in a light brown sunburst. The top was made of spruce and had a reproduction of Red Foley's signature with the inscription "Smooth Trailin" painted on in cream color along with a cowboy hat painted in brown. The long triangular tortoise shell colored pickguard had an art deco decoration painted in cream color. The ebonized pin bridge had a bone saddle with white pins. The top edge of the body had white celluloid binding. The back and sides were made of maple. The neck had an ebonized fretboard with four mother-of-pearl inlaid position dots. The peghead had a very square shape and was simply painted black with no brand name shown. The guitar came with a 95-page Red Foley songbook, a pick, and a braided neck cord - all for $8.95.

**Spring of 1943 "Red Foley" signature model guitar, concert size, 37 3/4" long, sunburst spruce top, tortoise shell colored pickguard, made by Harmony, sold through Wards.**

**Circa early 1940's "Red Foley" scene guitar, 36 3/4" long, diamond designs painted on peghead and fretboard, old style trapeze tailpiece with hidden string attachment, made by Richter.**

Circa early 1940's "Red Foley" scene shows a cowboy on horseback
with stream, trees and mountains in background, sunburst birch
body with scene painted in white and bright blue, white striping.

November 1940 cowboy guitar made
by Richter, long trapeze tailpiece.

November 1940 cowboy guitar, gray
with scene painted in black, similar
scene to the "Red Foley" scene guitar.

Red Foley, far left, leads the Ozark Jubilee cast.

# RED FOLEY

Clyde Julian "Rambling Red" Foley, called the "Bing Crosby of the Hillbillies," one of the all-time country greats, had a number of 'firsts' to his name. He was the first country star to have a radio network show; he hosted one of the first successful country TV series; he was the first country star to actually record in Nashville; and was one of the first singers to record more that a million sales with gospel music. Most people think Red is a native of Kentucky. Actually he was born in Tucumcari, New Mexico on June 17,1910. As a small boy the Foleys moved to Kentucky and settled on a farm near Berea, where Red grew up.

He was a star athlete at high school and college. In1930 he moved to Chicago to join the John Lair's Cumberland Ridge Runners, a string band that sparkled with individual talent and was a staple ingredient of the WLS National Barn Dance. They were one of the first bands to incorporate a square dance group. Years later Foley and Lair helped to originate the Renfro Valley Show and in 1939 appeared on *Avalon Time*, a program in which he co-starred with comedian Red Skelton. During the 1940s he was a regular at the Grand Ole Opry, and in 1954 was invited to host the *Ozark Jubilee Show* from Springfield, Missouri, on ABC TV. He was a regular on the ABC TV series *Mr. Smith Goes to Washington*, in the early 1960s. He had a long string of hit records with Decca records including *Candy Kisses*, *Chattanooga Shoe Shine Boy*, and *Peace in the Valley*.

Red Foley was an outstanding pioneer of the modern country sound. He continued appearing on radio and TV and making many personal appearances right up to the time of his death on September 19, 1968, in Fort Wayne, Indiana.

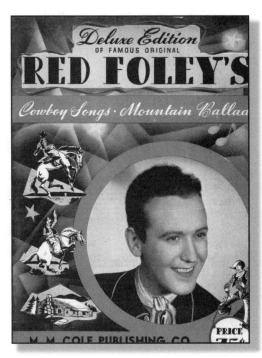

**1941 Songbook**

**1949 Songbook**

# "PRAIRIE RAMBLERS" GUITAR

## as Sold by
## Spiegel

From the spring of 1942 through the spring of 1966, intermittently, Spiegel offered the "Prairie Ramblers" guitar.
This model was made for Spiegel by the Kay Musical Instrument Company. Kay also sold variations of the same guitar to other distributors, but Spiegel was their largest outlet.

The "Prairie Ramblers" scene showed a cowboy music group. Today, some guitar collectors refer to this model as the "Bunkhouse Orchestra". The whole scene was positioned at the lower portion of the guitar. Four cowboys playing their instruments – banjo, bass fiddle, mandolin and guitar – were shown sitting around a fire. Also in the scene was a stagecoach and in the background, a bunkhouse.

**Early 1940's Del Oro "Prairie Ramblers" light brown sunburst finish with white scene and white striping, grand concert size, (36 1/2" X 14 1/2"), white pickguard, made by Kay, note trapeze tailpiece with hidden string attachment.**

**Circa 1958 Old Kraftsman "Prairie Ramblers" sometimes referred to as "Bunkhouse Orchestra", chocolate brown guitar with white scene, solid trapeze tailpiece with raised center.**

When the "Prairie Ramblers" guitar was first introduced in the spring of 1942, it had the "Del Oro" brand name painted on the squared-off peghead. It was a grand concert size (36 1/2" X 14 1/2") guitar made of birch, finished in light brown sunburst with a white scene and with top edge and soundhole striping painted in white. The first issue came with a black pickguard attached by two wood screws. The ebonized fretboard had four mother-of-pearl dot inlays and 12 frets clear of the body. The trapeze tailpiece had hidden string attachment and a moveable wooden bridge. With this guitar, Spiegel included three initials (pick shaped decals), neck cord, pick, and "Prairie Ramblers Barn Dance Favorites" songbook – all for the reasonable price of $6.98. One could also receive a canvas case and Hawaiian conversion kit for an additional $3.00.

Spiegel dropped the "Prairie Ramblers" model from the line from fall of 1942 through the spring of 1955. When it showed up again in the 1955 fall catalog, several changes had occurred. The brand name painted on the more shapely peghead had changed from "Del Oro" to "Old Kraftsman". Instead of a trapeze tailpiece, it had a glued-on wooden bridge. It now had fourteen frets clear of the body and the fretboard had been changed from ebonized to walnut. The now maple body guitar had different measurements (38 1/4" X 13 1/2") and there was no pickguard. By this time the three initials and the Hawaiian kit had been discontinued.

Circa 1950's Kamico "Prairie Ramblers" brown guitar with white scene, fourteen frets clear of the body, triangular shaped white pickguard, made by Kay.

113

By the fall of 1956 the "Prairie Ramblers" was coming with a trapeze tailpiece that was solid with a raised portion outlining where the opening would be on a traditional trapeze. The 1957 spring catalog showed yet another trapeze tailpiece that was hourglass-shaped with sculptured edges.

By the fall of 1958 the guitar's finish had been changed to a chocolate brown color with white striping around the top and back edges and soundhole, and the trapeze tailpiece had changed back to the solid type with raised portion. Spiegel's catalog described the guitar as "Ideal for beginners, but also an all-purpose instrument that you can take with you on picnics, beach parties and auto trips".

In the spring of 1959 the finish was changed to a dark brown sunburst with flame maple effect. The fretboard was made of maple with six painted on black rectangle position markers. This model was advertised as having a steel reinforced neck.

By the spring of 1962 a pickguard had been added, but in the fall of 1962 the real pickguard was replaced by a stencil painted pickguard. In the spring of 1963 the tailpiece was changed to a true hinged trapeze tailpiece, but in the fall of 1963 it was changed back to the old hourglass-shaped trapeze tailpiece. By this time the "Prairie Ramblers" guitar was coming with a bolt-on neck instead of the traditional glued-on neck and the stenciled pickguard has disappeared.

By the fall of 1965 the trapeze tailpiece had been changed to a new shiny style with no raised portion. This final version remained until the spring of 1966. By the fall of 1966 the "Prairie Ramblers" had been permanently discontinued.

**1951 Songbook**

**Mid 1960's Old Kraftsman "Prairie Ramblers" dark brown sunburst with maple flame painted on, bolt-on neck, made by Kay, sold through Spiegel.**

**Circa 1960's Old Kraftsman "Prairie Ramblers" sunburst with white scene and white striping, painted-on black rectangle position markers.**

# THE PRAIRIE RAMBLERS

The Prairie Ramblers, long associated with WLS and the National Barn Dance, were one of the most influential of the early string bands. Their style progressed through the years from Southeast string band to western swing in their National Barn Dance tenure of 1932-56.

There were numerous personnel changes in the band throughout its life but the nucleus of the Ramblers was formed by Charles "Smiling Chick" Hurt - mandolin, tenor banjo and three of his neighbors in western Kentucky, Jack "Happy" Taylor - string bass, Shelby "Tex" Atchison - fiddle and Floyd "Salty" Holmes - guitar, harmonica, and jug.

Originally called the Kentucky Ramblers, they began on radio at WOC, in Davenport, Iowa, but within a few months were members of the National Barn Dance and changed their name to the Prairie Ramblers, where they teamed with Patsy Montana, backing her on her records and live performances. They introduced many important songs like *Feast Here Tonight*, *Shady Grove* and *Rolling On*.

As time went on, however, their style became increasingly swingy. An interesting note – they also recorded a number of risqué songs under the name of the Sweet Violet Boys.

Atchison left the band in 1937, heading for California, where he appeared in many films and with the bands of Jimmy Wakely, Ray Whitley, Merle Travis and others. Holmes left and returned, then went on to a career that took him to the Grand Ole Opry with his wife Maddie (Martha Carson's sister) as "Salty and Maddie." Atchison was replaced by Alan Crockett, who shot himself in 1947. Crockett was replaced by Wade Ray, and Wade was replaced by Wally Moore. The band finally ground to a halt in 1956. Hurt and Taylor (the original members) were playing with a polka band, Stan Wallowick And His Polka Chips, which they continued to do for nearly another decade.

They recorded for the ARC complex of labels, Conqueror, Vocalion, Okeh, Mercury, Victor and Bluebird. Recordings were also issued under the name Blue Ridge Ramblers.

**The Prairie Ramblers from a 1938 WLS Family Album. From the left, Tex Atchison, Salty Holmes, Chick Hurt, Jack Taylor.**

**The Prairie Ramblers and Patsy Montana. Patsy had the first female million selling record, *I Want To Be A Cowboy's Sweetheart*.**

# "POWDER RIVER, JACK LEE" GUITAR

## as Sold by

## Simpsons, Limited (Made in Canada)

From the spring of 1942 through the spring of 1946, Simpson's offered a "Powder River, Jack Lee" model guitar. The standard size (37" X 13 1/4") birch guitar had a shaded brown (sunburst) finish with a scene painted in black and green.

The scene showed a cowboy on horseback riding toward a distant butte. On the left of the body was a cactus and on the upper right the words "Powder River" and a reproduction of Jack Lee's signature was painted in green. The 1942 model had a nickel-plated trapeze style tailpiece (resembling the early "Plainsman" cowboy guitar tailpiece) and a thin moveable wooden bridge. The neck was ebonized and had three inlaid position dots. The first version had geared machine tuners, but in 1943 the "Powder River, Jack Lee" started coming with wooden

violin-style tuning pegs. At the same time the tailpiece changed to a newer style trapeze tailpiece that was painted black. The 1943 (war era) model came with a label inside that described how to keep the wooden tuning pegs in tune and explained how the use of metal in civilian articles was severely restricted. By 1946 the geared tuning machines were back in use.

**Circa 1943 "Powder River, Jack Lee" standard size 37" long, three position dots inlaid in ebonized fretboard, birch body, gun metal black trapeze tailpiece, note wooden violin style tuning pegs, made in Canada, sold through Simpson's. Brown sunburst with scene painted in black and green, label inside guitar reads "The use of metal in civilian articles is now severely restricted" and goes on to describe how to keep the tuning pegs in tune, states "This is a war necessity".**

# JACK H. "POWDER RIVER" AND KITTY LEE

This couple was one of the most colorful duets in western music. They were the first to record the popular *Sierry Petes* (*Tying A Knot in the Devil's Tail*), written by Gail Gardner and set to music by Bill Simon. Jack Lee claimed that he wrote it, as well as other traditional cowboy songs such as *Powder River, Let'er Buck*. However, he was not the only one to claim authorship of old songs. He may have written some of them.

Jack was a real cowboy who, in his early youth, herded droves of longhorns along the Chisholm Trail. He was with Buffalo Bill's Wild West Show where he won admiration at home and abroad as an ideal representative of the western cowpuncher and bronco buster. Kitty Lee, his lifelong partner, was the lady who did the trick riding with Colonel Cody's Wild West organization on its worldwide tour. They appeared on the scene when cowboy songs grew popular. By 1930, Jack was billed as "Montana's Cowboy Poet." He is the author of the book, *West of Powder River*, containing cowboy songs and poems. He owned the Deer Lodge ranch in Montana.

His rugged features, cast in bronze, adorn the Palace of Education at the San Diego Exposition as the *Trio of Famous American Cowboys*, along with Will Rogers and Charles M. Russell.

**Powder River Jack and Kitty Lee entertaining the cowboys at the Calgary Stampede, 1932.**

**1937**

117

# "BUCKIN' BRONCO" GUITAR
## as Sold by
## T. Eaton Company

From the summer of 1943 through the summer of 1946, Eatons offered a "Buckin' Bronco" guitar. The standard size (37" X 13 1/4") birch guitar had a natural finished top with back and sides stained walnut color. The scene was painted black and white and showed a cowboy waiving his hat in the air while riding a bucking horse. It was a real action scene with the horse jumping high into the air. There was a bit of prairie grass and some distant mountains also shown. The 1943 model had a slotted peghead with wooden friction (violin type) tuning pegs. A label inside the guitar explained how the use of metal in civilian articles was severely restricted and also gave some tips for tuning the wooden pegs. The fretboard was ebonized and had three inlaid white dot position markers. The moveable wooden bridge was also ebonized and the metal tailpiece was painted black. By the summer of 1946 the "Buckin' Bronco" guitar was coming with geared tuning machines instead of wooden tuning pegs.

Circa late 1940's "Buckin' Bronco" with big fence shown in scene, natural finish with scene painted in black and tan, slotted peghead, black metal trapeze tailpiece, made in Canada.

Circa 1943 "Buckin' Bronco" guitar, this is an early model that does not have a fence shown in the scene, natural finish with black and white scene, made in Canada, sold through Eaton.

**The label inside the 1943 model.
Notice after the tuning tips it says
"This is a War NECESSITY"**

The "Buckin' Bronco" guitar came with several accessories, including six songbooks (one was a large Gene Autry book), two instruction books and a Hawaiian conversion kit consisting of an extension nut, slide bar, thumb pick and two finger picks. The total outfit price was $7.95 Canadian. A late 1940's variation of the "Buckin' Bronco" guitar, sold through an outlet other than Eatons, had the same bucking bronc scene, but instead of distant mountains, it had a big fence with four cowboys watching the action. Instead of black and white, the scene was painted black and tan. On a still later version of the "Buckin' Bronco with Big Fence" guitar, the colors of the scene had been changed to black and red, and the guitar came with a shiny metal tailpiece and a more modern non-slot peghead.

**1960 "Buckin' Bronco" with big fence in scene, natural finish with scene painted in black and red, solid peghead, shiny metal trapeze tailpiece, made in Canada.**

119

# "PIONEER DAYS" STYLE SCENE
## as Sold by
## Montgomery Ward

From the fall of 1949 through the spring of 1954, Wards offered their version of the "Pioneer Days". This guitar, made by Harmony for Wards, did not have the name "Pioneer Days" painted on the guitar. The scene showed a wagon train with mountains, clouds, and a sunset off in the distance. The scene was painted in tan and cream with a small patch of green. White striping was painted around the top edge of the body and the soundhole. The standard size (36" X 13") guitar had an all birch body finished in brown sunburst. The strings attached to a nickel-plated tailpiece with heart cutouts and crossed over a moveable wooden bridge. The ebonized fretboard was inlaid with five large square position markers.

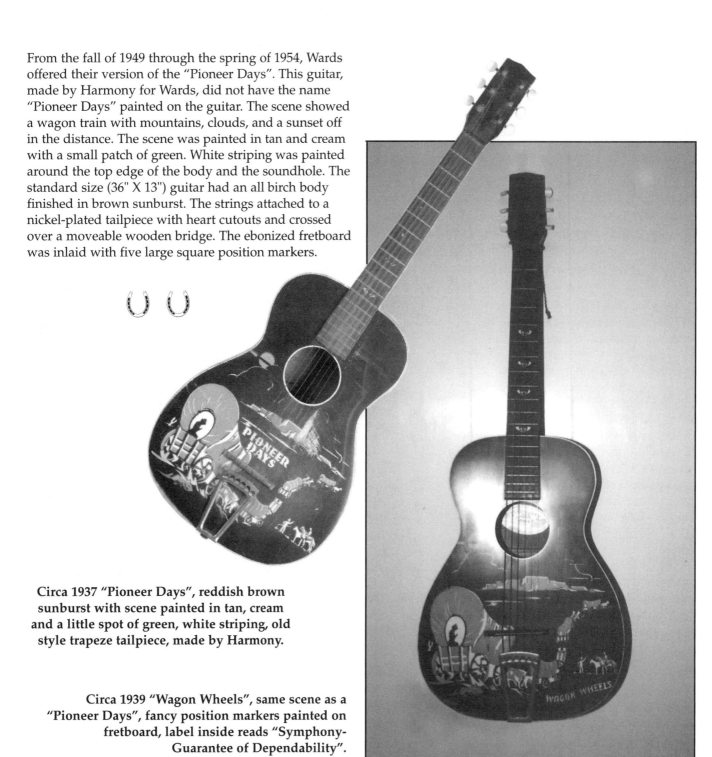

**Circa 1937 "Pioneer Days", reddish brown sunburst with scene painted in tan, cream and a little spot of green, white striping, old style trapeze tailpiece, made by Harmony.**

**Circa 1939 "Wagon Wheels", same scene as a "Pioneer Days", fancy position markers painted on fretboard, label inside reads "Symphony-Guarantee of Dependability".**

By the spring of 1950 the fretboard had been changed to a rosewood color, and the position markers were three Harmony style (triple-bar sandwich) markers painted on in white.

For the year of 1952, Wards did not offer the "Pioneer Days" style guitar, but an improved version was back in the lineup in the spring of 1953. It came with a spruce top and real binding around the top edge and soundhole. By late 1954 the "Pioneer Days" style had been permanently dropped from the line.

The same "Pioneer Days" style scene had also been used on a guitar with Harmony painted on the peghead, circa 1939 and the name "Wagon Wheels" painted on the lower right-hand portion of the scene. This was a standard size guitar finished in brown sunburst with white striping painted on the top edge and around the soundhole. The ebonized fretboard was stenciled with fancy position markers. The strings attached to a nickel-plated "old style" trapeze tailpiece and crossed over a moveable wooden bridge.

Circa 1949 "Pioneer Days" style scene, inlaid block position markers, brown sunburst finish, made by Harmony, sold through Wards.

Early 1950's "Pioneer Days" style, but no name shown on body, brown sunburst finish with scene painted in tan, cream and green, white striping painted on top edge.

1951 "Pioneer Days", name on body,
brown sunburst birch body with wagon train
scene painted in tan, cream and green,
made by Harmony.

Circa 1953-1954 "Pioneer Days" style guitar, spruce
top with real binding on top edge and soundhole.
This guitar is easy to spot as being made by Harmony
because of the tailpiece and the "Harmony" style
painted-on position markers, sold through Wards.

# "PIONEER DAYS"/"WAGON TRAIN" GUITAR
## as Sold by
## Simpsons-Sears Limited (Made in Canada)

During the spring of 1940 and again in 1962 through 1963, Simpsons-Sears offered a Canadian-made guitar with a wagon train scene painted on the body. This scene was a reproduction of a scene used on some guitars produced by Harmony Company of Chicago, IL. The scene was painted in red and white and showed a wagon train with mountains, clouds and a sunset off in the distance. This standard size (36 1/2" X 13 1/4") birch guitar usually came in brown sunburst and can be found with either the name "Pioneer Days" or "Wagon Train" painted just above the bridge.

Circa 1960 "Wagon Train" guitar, made in Canada, black finish with scene in red and white, nickel-plated trapeze tailpiece.

Circa 1961 "Wagon Train", made in Canada, scene is very similar to the "Pioneer Days" made by Harmony.

For the spring of 1940 Simpsons offered a "Pioneer Days" guitar. The guitar advertised in the catalog was shown with a reverse scene. Apparently the scene had been painted using a stencil that had been flipped over on its other side. This guitar had an ebonized pin bridge and an ebonized fretboard with three position dots. It also had the old style squared-off slotted peghead.

During the spring of 1962 through Christmas of 1963, Simpson-Sears offered a "Wagon Train" guitar. It was the same guitar as the "Pioneer Days" except for the name and a few modern changes, such as a non-slot peghead and a shiny metal tailpiece with moveable wooden bridge.

**Circa early 1960's "Wagon Train" guitar, made in Canada, brown sunburst with scene in red and white, three position dots, shiny trapeze tailpiece.**

# "ROY ROGERS AND TRIGGER, HAPPY TRAILS" GUITAR
## as Sold by
## Simpsons, Limited (Made in Canada)

During the spring of 1951 Simpson's offered a "Roy Rogers" guitar. The standard size (36 1/2" X 13 1/4") birch guitar had a natural-finished top with a red and gold scene and a shaded back and sides. The guitar had a shiny metal tailpiece and moveable wooden bridge. The fretboard was ebonized and had three position dots, and the peghead was slotted. The scene was very elaborate. On the left was Roy Rogers riding Trigger in true hero fashion with Trigger reared up on hind legs.

Simpson's spring and summer 1951 catalog from Toronto shows a "Roy Rogers" and a "Wilf Carter" model, both made in Canada.

1951 "Roy Rogers" guitar made in Canada, natural finished birch top with red and gold scene, dark stained back and sides, slotted peghead, sold through Simpson's.

To the right was a cactus, and in the distance were mesas and cloudy skies. At the top of the scene were the words "Happy Trails" spelled out in rope letters. To the right and just below the soundhole were the words "Roy Rogers and Trigger", Roy's name being spelled out in rope letters. Included with the guitar was a neck cord, flat pick, two instruction books, a cowboy song book, an extra set of strings, and Hawaiian accessories including an extension nut, slide bar and finger picks – all for $14.95 Canadian, delivered. I'll take one.

**1953 Canadian made "Roy Rogers" guitar, this style predates the American made "Roy Rogers" by Harmony.**

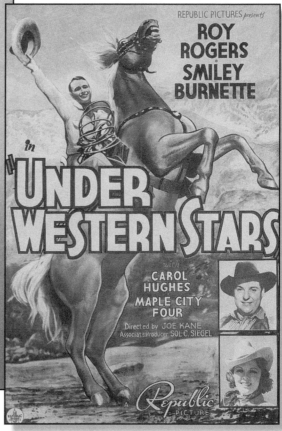

**1938 Movie poster**

# NEWER STYLE "ROY ROGERS"
## Canadian Guitar

Circa 1956 through 1958 a new "Roy Rogers" guitar was made in Canada. It was a standard-size birch guitar like the 1951 model offered by Simpson's but had a different scene. The scene was a reproduction of the "Roy Rogers" guitar being made in the USA by Harmony. It showed Roy Rogers sitting cross-legged and playing guitar next to a campfire, with Roy's horse, Trigger, in the background. Also shown were distant trees and mountains. In 1956 the "Roy Rogers" was available with a natural satin-finished top with a dark brown and tan scene. In 1958 it came with a very dark satin finish with scene painted in tan and ivory.

The scene looked very similar to the American version, but other features identify the guitar as made in Canada, such as the color and type of finish, the shape of the peghead, the three dot position markers, and the metal tailpiece - all common features of Canadian cowboy guitars from the 50's and early 60's.

1958 "Roy Rogers" guitar, made in Canada, dark finish with scene painted in tan and ivory. The three dot position markers and trapeze tailpiece helps identify as made in Canada.

1956 Canadian-made "Roy Rogers" guitar in natural finished birch with scene in dark brown and tan, scene resembles the US made "Roy Rogers".

# "ROY ROGERS" GUITAR
## as Sold by
## Sears, Roebuck & Co.

From the fall of 1954 through the spring of 1958, Sears offered the "Roy Rogers" guitar. This model was made for Sears by the Harmony Company of Chicago. It featured a Western scene, painted in brown and bright yellow, which depicted Roy Rogers playing guitar by a campfire and his horse Trigger standing in the background. The name Roy Rogers is painted at the bottom of the scene and is also painted up on the peghead, where there is a small caricature of Roy Roger's face. The guitar had a shaded brown (sunburst) finish. The body of the guitar was made of birch. A white stripe was painted around the soundhole and the top edges of the body, which gave the look of binding and help "set off" the guitar. The bridge was advertised as a "new type" pinless bridge. The ebonized fretboard had four inlaid white position dots and a string nut made of wood. The tuning keys were three-on-a-side plank style with white plastic tuning buttons.

**Likeness of Roy Rogers' face and signature on the peghead of this 1956 3/4 size "Roy Rogers" model.**

**1956 "Roy Rogers" 3/4 size, 32" long, sunburst finish with brown and bright yellow scene, birch body, made by Harmony, sold through Sears, note pinless bridge.**

**Roy Rogers playing his signature guitar.**

The Sears 1954 fall catalog stated "Endorsed by Roy Rogers 'King of the Cowboys', its 3/4 size (11" X 32") makes it easy for 'young cowhands' to hold and play". The guitar's price of $12.95 included an instruction booklet, braided neck cord and a pick. A Western design case was available for $4.00 extra.

In the fall of 1955 Sears offered the Roy Rogers in two sizes: the 3/4 size and a "standard" size (13" X 36"). Besides being larger, the standard size was a bit of an upgrade over the 3/4 size. It had a spruce top with maple back and sides and also had real binding around the soundhole and on the top edge of the body. The larger "standard" size was only available from the fall of 1955 through the spring of 1957. The original 3/4 size Roy Rogers continued to be available through the spring of 1958. The last advertisement for the Roy Rogers wooden guitar was seen on page 872 of Sears 1958 spring catalog. On that same page, just below the Roy Rogers guitar was an offering for an Elvis Presley song book, and page 874 featured the new Silvertone/Dan Electro electric guitars suited for the rock & roll music of a new generation of youngsters.

Roy "Dusty" Rogers Jr. on the 1961 sheet music cover of "Silver Bells", holding the 3/4 size "Roy Rogers" guitar.

Mid 1950's 3/4 size "Roy Rogers" sunburst with white striping painted around top edge and soundhole, original neck cord and Western design case.

Roy Sr. showing Roy Jr. some chords.

Mid 1950's "Roy Rogers" standard size, 36" long, spruce top with maple
back and sides, real binding, note 1950's Roy Rogers lamp in background.

# "ROY ROGERS" FIBERBOARD GUITARS

## as Sold by
## Sears, Roebuck & Co.

Besides the all wood models, Sears also offered a very low priced Roy Rogers guitar made of fiberboard – fiberboard being equivalent to a very strong cardboard. Many people consider these fiberboard models as toys. However, they were actual working guitars. From 1956 through 1974, Sears offered five different versions; each priced below $5.00. All five were made with a fiberboard body and wood neck, but had different Roy Rogers scenes. Four of the five scenes were "set off" with a white rope design that outlined the front of the body and each had a big "Roy Rogers" signature at the lower bout. The first three issues were made by the Rich Toy Company, which had factories in Chicago, Illinois, and Tupelo, Mississippi, and usually had a label on the peghead that read "A Range Rhythm Toy". The fourth and fifth issues usually had a shiny gold stick-on label identifying them as made by the Jefferson Manufacturing Company of Philadelphia, Pennsylvania.

1.  The first issue, offered from Christmas 1956 through Christmas 1958, was a bright red guitar with white (single color) artwork. On the lower portion of the guitar's front was a picture of Roy Rogers on his horse Trigger who is reared up. A fence and entranceway to the "Roy Rogers Double R Bar Ranch" are also depicted. At the upper bout, a mountain and clouds are on the left and a branding iron on the right side. The 1956 model had a wood fretboard with metal frets, but in 1958 this was changed to a plastic fretboard with raised plastic frets. The guitar measured 11 1/8" at the lower bout by 30 3/8" in total length. When Sears first advertised this model in the 1956 Christmas catalog, it was shown next to the Roy Rogers harmonica in the toy section.

2.  The second issue offered from Christmas 1959 through Christmas 1961 was very similar to the first issue. The guitar was still red with the scene done in white, but the artwork had been redone. The mountains and clouds on the upper left bout had been replaced by a picture of Roy's face. The rest of the scene resembled the first issue, but with more clarity. The artwork, however, looks less professional on the second issue.

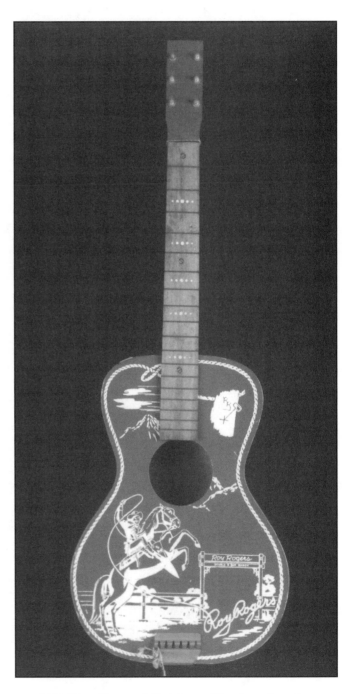

**1956 "Roy Rogers" first issue fiberboard guitar, Range Rhythm Toys, bright red with scene in white, note wooden fretboard with metal frets.**

Copyright 1957 plastic Roy Rogers guitar, 20" long, black guitar with gold foil applique, made by Reliable Plastic Company of Toronto, Canada.

Peghead of 1958 fiberboard "Roy Rogers", sold through Sears.

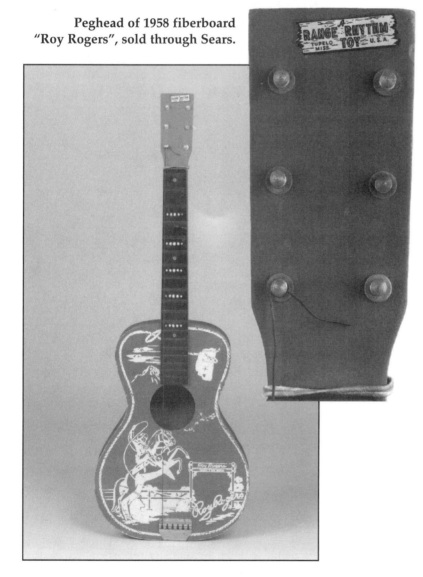

1958 "Roy Rogers" fiberboard guitar with original hang tags, Range Rhythm Toy, made by Rich Toy Company who had factories in Chicago, Illinois and in Tupelo, Mississippi.

1958 "Roy Rogers" fiberboard guitar, 30 3/8" long, note plastic fretboard with molded frets.

1943 Songbook

Circa 1959-1961 "Roy Rogers" second issue fiberboard guitar with original shipping carton, bright red with white scene, made in Tupelo, Mississippi by Rich Toy Company.

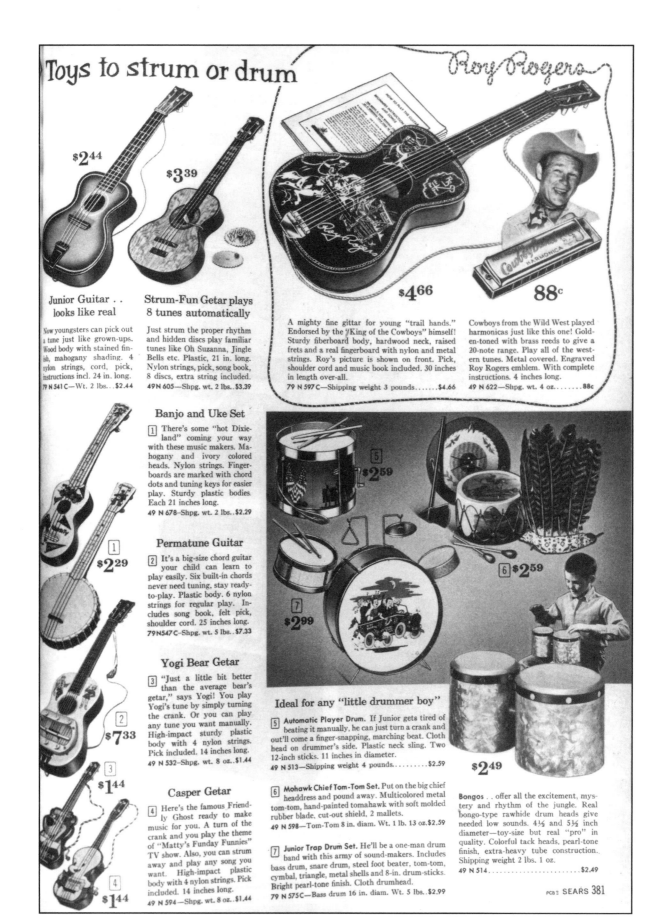

# Toys to strum or drum

*Roy Rogers*

### $2⁴⁴

**Junior Guitar . . looks like real**

Now youngsters can pick out a tune just like grown-ups. Wood body with stained finish, mahogany shading. 4 nylon strings, cord, pick, instructions incl. 24 in. long.
79 N 541 C—Wt. 2 lbs . . $2.44

### $3³⁹

**Strum-Fun Getar plays 8 tunes automatically**

Just strum the proper rhythm and hidden discs play familiar tunes like Oh Suzanna, Jingle Bells etc. Plastic, 21 in. long. Nylon strings, pick, song book, 8 discs, extra string included.
49 N 605—Shpg. wt. 2 lbs . . $3.39

### $4⁶⁶

A mighty fine gittar for young "trail hands." Endorsed by the "King of the Cowboys" himself! Sturdy fiberboard body, hardwood neck, raised frets and a real fingerboard with nylon and metal strings. Roy's picture is shown on front. Pick, shoulder cord and music book included. 30 inches in length over-all.
79 N 597 C—Shipping weight 3 pounds . . . . . . $4.66

### 88ᶜ

Cowboys from the Wild West played harmonicas just like this one! Golden-toned with brass reeds to give a 20-note range. Play all of the western tunes. Metal covered. Engraved Roy Rogers emblem. With complete instructions. 4 inches long.
49 N 622—Shpg. wt. 4 oz . . . . . . 88c

### Banjo and Uke Set

[1] There's some "hot Dixieland" coming your way with these music makers. Mahogany and ivory colored heads. Nylon strings. Fingerboards are marked with chord dots and tuning keys for easier play. Sturdy plastic bodies. Each 21 inches long.
49 N 678—Shpg. wt. 2 lbs . . $2.29

### Permatune Guitar

[2] It's a big-size chord guitar your child can learn to play easily. Six built-in chords never need tuning, stay ready-to-play. Plastic body. 6 nylon strings for regular play. Includes song book, felt pick, shoulder cord. 25 inches long.
79 N 547 C–Shpg. wt. 5 lbs . . $7.33

### Yogi Bear Getar

[3] "Just a little bit better than the average bear's getar," says Yogi! You play Yogi's tune by simply turning the crank. Or you can play any tune you want manually. High-impact sturdy plastic body with 4 nylon strings. Pick included. 14 inches long.
49 N 532—Shpg. wt. 8 oz . . $1.44

### Casper Getar

[4] Here's the famous Friendly Ghost ready to make music for you. A turn of the crank and you play the theme of "Matty's Funday Funnies" TV show. Also, you can strum away and play any song you want. High-impact plastic body with 4 nylon strings. Pick included. 14 inches long.
49 N 594—Shpg. wt. 8 oz . . $1.44

**$2²⁹** [1]
**$7³³** [2]
**$1⁴⁴** [3]
**$1⁴⁴** [4]

### Ideal for any "little drummer boy"

**[5] $2⁵⁹**
**[6] $2⁵⁹**
**[7] $2⁹⁹**

[5] **Automatic Player Drum.** If Junior gets tired of beating it manually, he can just turn a crank and out'll come a finger-snapping, marching beat. Cloth head on drummer's side. Plastic neck sling. Two 12-inch sticks. 11 inches in diameter.
49 N 513—Shipping weight 4 pounds . . . . . . . . $2.59

[6] **Mohawk Chief Tom-Tom Set.** Put on the big chief headdress and pound away. Multicolored metal tom-tom, hand-painted tomahawk with soft molded rubber blade, cut-out shield, 2 mallets.
49 N 598—Tom-Tom 8 in. diam. Wt. 1 lb. 13 oz. $2.59

[7] **Junior Trap Drum Set.** He'll be a one-man drum band with this army of sound-makers. Includes bass drum, snare drum, steel foot beater, tom-tom, cymbal, triangle, metal shells and 8-in. drum-sticks. Bright pearl-tone finish. Cloth drumhead.
79 N 575 C—Bass drum 16 in. diam. Wt. 5 lbs . . $2.99

**$2⁴⁹**

**Bongos** . . offer all the excitement, mystery and rhythm of the jungle. Real bongo-type rawhide drum heads give needed low sounds. 4½ and 5½ inch diameter—toy-size but real "pro" in quality. Colorful tack heads, pearl-tone finish, extra-heavy tube construction. Shipping weight 2 lbs. 1 oz.
49 N 514 . . . . . . . . . . . . . . . . . . . . . . $2.49

Sears Christmas 1961 catalog shows the second variation of red "Roy Rogers" fiberboard guitar with new artwork.

3. The third issue was offered only in Sears' Christmas 1962 catalog. The body of the guitar was bright yellow with the artwork done in blue, red and black. This model is peculiar in that the artwork shows cartoon-like children as cowboys and cowgirls. It would be hard to know this model was a Roy Rogers guitar if not for the Roy Rogers signature. The guitar measured 10 7/8" at the lower bout by 30 3/4" in total length. It had a wooden neck with a black plastic fretboard with raised frets.

Roy, Trigger and Dale.

1962 "Roy Rogers" fiberboard guitar, bright yellow with juvenile cowboy scenes, Range Rhythm label. This model was available in the Christmas 1962 Sears catalog.

## Dale Evans, Queen of the West

Dale was born Frances Smith, at Ulvalda, Texas on October 31, 1912. Brought up in Texas and Arkansas, attending high school in the latter state, Dale married Thomas Fox in 1928. She and her husband parted two years later–at which time she began concentrating on a career as a popular vocalist.

During the 1930's she became a band singer with the Anson Weeks Orchestra, then became resident vocalist on the CBS News and Rhythm Show, followed by many appearances on major radio shows. In 1942 Dale started appearing in such film productions as "Orchestra Wives"; 1943, "Swing Your Partner"; 1944, "The Cowboy and the Senorita", the first of many with Roy Rogers.

Dale became America's favorite cowgirl after fate hitched her wagon to Roy Rogers. "Before I realized what was happening," recalled Evans, "I was typecast as a Western player." She married Roy in 1947.

She recorded several records with Roy. She wrote one of the most popular western songs, "Happy Trails", and "The Bible Tells Me So", one of the most famous American hymns. Dale was the author of more than 20 inspirational books. The Queen of the West passed away at age 88 on February 7, 2001.

4. The fourth issue, offered from Christmas 1963 through 1965, had an orange sunburst on front and back, with orange colored sides. The Sears catalog described the guitar as "an ivory color with rich maple-toned shadings". The picture on the guitar shows Roy Rogers riding Trigger. On the upper left is a picture of Roy Roger's face and on the upper right is a picture of Dale Evans' face. According to the 1963 catalog, the artwork was printed on the guitar with black and white ink. By 1965 the same picture was being printed on the guitar with brown and white ink. The wooden neck had an attached fretboard (with raised frets) made of fiberboard. The fretboard was black with yellow frets and position dots. The guitar measured 10 3/4" at the lower bout by 28 3/4" in total length.

**Circa 1964 "Roy Rogers", fourth issue fiberboard guitar, orange to cream sunburst with scene in brown and white, made by Jefferson Manufacturing of Philadelphia, Pennsylvania, sold through Sears.**

**Circa 1966 through 1974 "Roy Rogers" fiberboard guitars, fifth issue, on left is a circa 1966 model with Roy Roger's signature in brown and longer tailpiece, early 1970's smaller model on right with white Roy Rogers' signature and short tailpiece, made by Jefferson, sold through Sears.**

5. The fifth issue, offered from Christmas 1966 through Christmas 1974, had the same orange sunburst coloring, as did the fourth issue. The scene on this model is placed more horizontally on the guitar's body – this way it is best viewed when the guitar is held in the playing position. The artwork was made up of a large picture of Roy Rogers standing beside his horse Trigger, a small picture of Dale Evans' face on the upper left, and a picture of a branding iron on the upper right. The artwork was printed on the guitar with brown and white ink. This fifth version of the "Roy Rogers" fiberboard guitar itself went through a few slight changes that can help to identify the model as being early or late in production tenure. In1966 the guitar measured 10 3/4" at the lower bout by 28 1/2" in total length, had a brown "Roy Rogers" signature, and had a 3" long tailpiece. By the early 1970's it was being produced in a slightly smaller size – 10 1/2" at the lower bout by 27 3/4" in total length, with a 2" long tailpiece and a white "Roy Rogers" signature. This same scene was still being produced by the manufacturer after Sears stopped carrying the guitar in the mid 1970's.

The five different scenes were artists drawings silk-screened on the guitars, but the fourth and fifth issues' scenes were so realistic they looked almost like photographs.

Unusual "Roy Rogers" guitar by Jefferson (with no Roy Rogers signature) made in the late '70's after Sears no longer carried the Roy Rogers model.

# ROY ROGERS

Roy Rogers, once the number one ranked cowboy star at the box office for more than ten straight years, assured us that goodness prevails, bad guys always suffer the consequences, and happy trails could somehow be followed "till we meet again."

Born November 5, 1911 as Leonard Franklin Sly in Cincinnati and growing up in Duck Run, Ohio to musical parents, mom sang, played mandolin, dad played guitar. Leonárd's first guitar was a pawnshop find for $20, made by Aida Guitar Company.

During the Great Depression in 1930, trying to find the Promised Land, he moved with his family to California where his older married sister lived. He drove trucks and picked fruit in central California. The long journey from poverty to fame started when he was seeking a living within the music industry. He had brief stints with several different singing groups, later teaming up with Bob Nolan and Tim Spencer to form the Pioneer Trio. With the addition of Hugh and Karl Farr, they became the *Sons of the Pioneers*, the greatest of all Western vocal groups. Leonard was considered a master at cowboy yodeling. With the tight harmonies and backup by the Farr brothers, the Sons brought a new sophistication to cowboy music and set the standard for all who were to follow. Their songs became American classics. They appeared in westerns, on radio, made personal appearances and recorded for American Recording Corp. and Decca records.

The Sons were successful, but Sly had higher goals for himself. Working bit parts in movies under the name Dick Weston, he stumbled into a Republic Studios audition in 1937, almost by accident, walking in without invitation with a group of extras. His boyish good looks and horse riding background made him a serious contender for roles in the cowboy movies but it was his proven abilities as a singer and guitar player that made him star material.

In 1937, he married Grace Arlene Wilkins, got his first big solo break in films and a new name, Leroy Rogers (after Will Rogers). Len didn't like Leroy and shortened it to Roy. He replaced a striking Gene Autry in *Under Western Skies*, released in 1938, with his horse Trigger and his sidekicks George "Gabby" (you ole whipper-snapper) Hayes and Pat Brady. Roy rose to the occasion and his star rose.

In 1946 Arlene died suddenly from an embolism six days after son Dusty (Roy Jr.) was born. Dale Evans the ex-big band singer and his co-star helped the young widower with his grief. On December 31, 1947 they married, soon to become "America's Favorite Western Couple." When his film contract ended in 1951, he and Dale moved to TV with *The Roy Rogers Show* that lasted until 1957 with over a hundred episodes.

Like Gene Autry, Roy's accomplishments and business successes are far too many to even attempt to mention in this short tribute. He was one of California's most successful businessmen. At the peak of Roy and Dale's popularity in the '50s, they were second only to Disney in merchandise sales. For a time, Rogers image seemed to be everywhere.

Roy cut his last Western record entitled *Tribute* in 1991. Everyone in Nashville wanted to appear on it with him. Roy had many guitars but his favorite was a Gibson Super 400.

Roy, the "King of the Cowboys," rode down that happy trail for the last time on July 6, 1998, assured that we will meet again. His legacy will continue to live on in the hearts of his fans and in the Roy Rogers-Dale Evans Museum in Victorville, California among his unbelievable array of memorabilia, www.royrogers.com and the Happy Trails Children's Foundation, www.happytrails.org.

# HORSE SENSE

Chivalry, that ten-dollar term that so many gentlemen have aspired to, ultimately has its roots in the five-franc French word cheval, meaning "horse." Mistreating a mare or a stallion was something a gentleman would never do. (Bringing it into a saloon was probably frowned upon, too.) Desperate settlers may have slit open their horses' bellies to tuck in their youngest children when caught in blizzards on the pioneer trail. Augustus Macrae of the television miniseries *Lonesome Dove* (1989) may have shot his horse in the head to make it a supine shield to bad men's bullets. Former NFL quarterback Alex Karras may have had the temerity to slug one in the chops in Mel Brooks' *Blazing Saddles* (1974). But a real gentleman treated his animal right.

Marlon Brando took things to an extreme (as he is wont to do) when he aimed stormy, romantic speeches at his horse, serenaded it with a harmonica, and shared a carrot with it (each eating from opposite ends and meeting in the middle) in Arthur Penn's *The Missouri Breaks* (1976), but his passion had a precedent. No self-respecting B western star was complete without his trusty steed, and many took the appreciation of horseflesh to a kind of reverence.

William S. Hart started it off by giving his horse, the first equine screen credit (*My Friend Flicka*, *Black Beauty*, and *Mr. Ed* would have approved), his own leading characters to play (*Pinto Ben*, 1915), and a kiss before dying (an act that gave cowboys the questionable reputation for romancing their horses instead of their sweethearts). Tom Mix graced his stallion with a love interest all his own in *Tumbling River* (1927) and star status in three more.*

Ken Maynard's horse could dance, roll over, play dead, even use his sense of smell to warn Ken when danger was coming. Maynard put his horse through incredible stunts – hanging virtually upside down from the horse's neck while at full gallop to grab a wounded man, or riding the steed off a sixty foot cliff into a lake (where the frightened horse tried to climb onto his master's shoulders). His horse often got better reviews than Ken: For *Lucky Larkin* (1930) *Variety* noted that "Next to Nora Larkin, ****** is the best actor in the film."

## Test Your Horse Sense

The following is a list of western movie, TV, and radio series stars and the marvelous mounts they rode. Some were show-biz stars in their own right. Some were just horses behind (or under) the men. (Some stars had horses with 2 or 3 different names, I picked the most famous). Match the horse with the rider, if you get them all correct you've been watching the Western Movie channel too much.

*Correct answers on page 227*

| Rider | Horse |
|---|---|
| William S. Hart | Mike |
| Tom Mix | Koko |
| Ken Maynard | Lucky |
| George O'Brien | Fritz |
| Hoot Gibson | Falcon |
| Buck Jones | Topper |
| Fred Thompson | Black Diamond |
| Colonel Tim McCoy | Champion |
| John Wayne | Rebel |
| Tex Ritter | Falcon |
| Jack Hoxie | Trazan the Wonder Horse |
| Buster Crabbe | Lightning |
| William "Hopalong Cassidy" Boyd | Diablo |
| Clayton "The Lone Ranger" Moore | White Eagle |
| Rex Allen | Topper |
| Lash Larue | Rush |
| Roy Rogers | Comet |
| Gene Autry | Scout |
| Dale Evans | War Paint |
| Duncan Renaldo "the Cisco Kid" | Silver King |
| Johnny Mack Brown | Duke |
| Jimmy Wakely | Tony |
| Eddie Dean | Buttermilk |
| Sunset Carson | Silver King |
| Joel McCrea "Texas Rangers" | Koko |
| Tim Holt | Silver |
| Brisco County Jr. | Mutt |
| Monte Hale | Cactus |

*(Source: Between a Rock, a Hard Place, and a Camera )*
*Tony Runs Wild (1926), Oh You, Tony (1924), and Just Tony

# KENNY ROBERTS "RUMBLIN' JR."
## Made by Harmony

The Kenny Roberts guitar and ukulele came out in 1950 when Kenny was a popular singing cowboy on radio and TV in Cincinnati, Ohio. The "Kenny Roberts, Rumblin' Jr." guitar was so named, because Kenny used to call his own guitar his "Rumbling Guitar." The uke was called the "Kenny Roberts, Little Pal" model because Kenny would refer to the children on his daily TV shows, as his "Little Pals." Both instruments were distributed by the Grossman Company out of Cleveland, Ohio, but were manufactured in Chicago, Illinois.

Circa 1950 Kenny Roberts "Little Pal" ukulele, light brown with scene in brown and peghead detail in white, spruce top and birch back, 21" long, made by Regal.

Circa 1950 Kenny Roberts "Rumblin' Jr." guitar made by Harmony. Sunburst finish guitar made of birch wood, with a picture of Kenny Roberts' face and the model name "Rumblin' Jr." painted on the guitar with

# KENNY ROBERTS

Kenny Roberts is celebrating over 50 years as a full time entertainer on stage, radio, records and TV. Kenny was born in Lenoir City, Tennessee in 1927. His first guitar was a Gene Autry guitar from a Sears catalog, paying $3.45 for it. He got his start doing daily radio and stage shows with the "Down Homers" western trio when he was 16 years old.

Throughout the years Roberts has recorded for several labels…Decca, Coral, Dot, King, Starday, Vogue, and Music Room. He started in 1946 with Vogue picture records and he was one of the very first country & western singers to reach the top 10 in the pop and country charts of Billboard and Variety with his million seller hit in 1949 on Coral records "I Never See Maggie Alone". His other hits include, *Chocolate Ice Cream Cone, Jealous Heart* and *Bluebird On Your Windowsill* and the yodelling extravaganzas, *Chime Bells* and *She Taught Me How To Yodel*. Roberts appeared and sang in the Gene Wilder and Richard Pryor movie "Another You". He has been featured on Grand Ole Opry, Hee Haw and several more top entertainment shows. A super yodeller billed as "King of the Yodellers" for over four decades. He continues to tour the U.S. and Europe with his singer, songwriter wife, Bettyanne.

Kenny Roberts

**Back left: Kenny Roberts, Bob Newbury, Ray Perkins. Front left: Blackie Newbury, Slim Clark. Radio station WHAI, Greenfield, Massachusetts, circa late 1930's.**

Label inside
soundhole of circa
1930s "Cowboy
Loye" model guitar.

Circa 1930s "Cowboy Loye" guitar, dark brown
stained birch guitar with white striping, trapeze
tailpiece, gold-sparkle inlaid position dots. "Cowboy
Loye" name painted in gold on peghead, 36 3/4" long.

Left, Just Plain John; right, Cowboy Loye

# COWBOY LOYE

Not much information could be found on Cowboy Loye. We do know his name as Loye D. Pack. Cowboy Loye was a radio star during the mid 1930s and early 1940s. We have photos of him behind the radio station mikes of WEEU and WWVA (West Virginia). There is a newspaper article dated May 30, 1993 from Morgantown, West Virginia. The article is about the history of a local flour mill company in that part of the country. It mentions Loye saying…Cowboy Lloyd (misspelled) a popular singer and disc jockey on local radio, made a deal with Wilhelm (the flour mill owner) to sell buckwheat flour. Lloyd would advertise the flour, if Wilhelm would buy sacks Lloyd provided. The brand name was *upper 10*. Mr. Wilhelm passed away March 1945.

One of his group photos (shown below right) shows Cowboy Loye behind a small suitcase, the sign saying "The Harping Sheep Herder and his 4 Harps, How Is Your Old Lady?" The "Sheep Herder" was the man standing on the far left; he played harmonica and fiddle, perhaps this was the band that backed Cowboy Loye on his radio programs.

We could find three songbooks with his name on them; *Heart Songs* and *Old Time Ballads & Cowboy Songs*, compiled by Cowboy Loye and Just Plain John, both small books with no copyright date or address and "Cowboy Loye's Simplified Guitar Method for Home Teaching" was his in cover only as it was really a Nick Manoloff guitar book (copyright 1935 by M. M. Cole publishing) with Cowboy Loye's own cover on it. Cowboy Loye must have had a mail order business, as he advertised it as "Cowboy Loye's Airway School of Music–a school dedicated to those interested in music selling musical instruments".

**Radio Station WWVA
Just Plain John, Custer Allen
and Cowboy Loye**

**Radio Station WEEU
Brother Bob, Cowboy Loye,
and Just Plain John**

# TEX MORTON

## Distributed by
## Tex Morton Music Warehouse, New Zealand

Mike Stevens owns this nice Tex Morton guitar, serial #6044, and took this photo with an original "Tex Morton" slide resting on the top. The distributor was in New Zealand, but the company who made it was Wayne Music, The Basin Ferntree Gully, Victoria, Australia.

Close up of the top and slide, Mike says this one is made with its top and back attached with tiny nails.
The label states:

100 pound
Guarantee
This is a Genuine
TEX MORTON GUITAR,
Serial No. 6044,
Super models also available
strings, music, accessories,
(crossed out is) Write Box 175B GPO Melbourne

This label states:

100 pound
Guarantee
This is a Genuine
TEX MORTON GUITAR
Serial No. 7295
TEX MORTON'S MUSIC WAREHOUSE,
P.O. Box
Symonds St., Auckland, NZ

The Tex Morton guitar came in a blond (cream) colored finish with black silk-screened art work. It has an ebonized bridge and fretboard. The extremely rare "Tex Morton" art work shows a cowboy on horseback throwing his lasso. The guitar body shape is similar to a Martin 000 size and is 38" in total length. The peghead has a red and gold insignia.

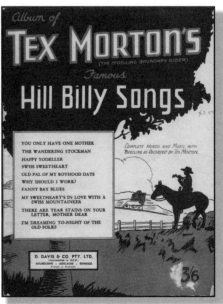

Tex Morton songbook, Published in Melbourne, Australia 1938

# TEX MORTON

Tex Morton's name has become synonymous with show business in Australia. The father of Australian Country Music and one of Australia's top selling Country & Western singers. Robert William Lane (Tex Morton) was actually born in Nelson, New Zealand, on August 30th 1916. He ran away from home at 14 and sang on street corners, in sideshows and with the occasional dance band. He came to Australia at the age of 16 in late 1932. In Australia he busked (singing on street corners), steeplejacked, was a drover and sheep shearer, did motor bike stunts in sideshows and even painted the Sydney Harbor Bridge.

A fine singer and yodeler, in 1936 he recorded his first songs for the Regal Zonophone label at the Homebush, Sydney, studios of The Columbia Gramophone Company, which sold very well. America's blue yodeler, Jimmie Rodgers, influenced Tex and his earliest songs were covers of American songs. A noted songwriter, eventually his own material came to be recognized, writing from an Australian point of view, in an Australian setting.

1937 found him touring with the Gladys Moncrief band and his records became hits. By 1943 he had cut 93 records. A favorite Tex Morton story illustrates how popular he was. A Melbourne charity came up with the idea of a penny trail down Bourke Street. Fans lined up pennies along the street as a test to who was the most popular. Tex Morton or Bing Crosby? Tex won!

In 1949 he moved to Canada and put together a circus-rodeo-singing, hypnotism show, touring Canada and the United States, billing himself as "the Great Morton – The World's Greatest Hypnotist", "Dr. Robert Morton", or "Sir Robert." He used "Robert Lane" in America as a personality of TV, radio and stage.

He returned to Australia in the 1960s and recorded through the 70s. His total song output was reported to be 300. He was one of the finest unofficial ambassadors for Australia. Tex died in Sydney in 1983.

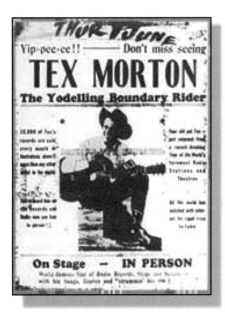

"The Yodelling Boundry Rider"
poster

"The Great Morton" poster

Tex Morton, left, shares the sheet music cover of the popular 1953 hit "Pistol Packin' Mama" with other Australian singers. From top, Bob Dyer, Smoke Dawson, and Smilin' Billy Blinkhorn.

# LEE MOORE

## Distributed by Tomchin Furniture Co.

**Lee Moore at WCHS Charleston, 1938.**

Walter LeRoy Moore had a significant career both as a traditional country musician and as a disc jockey. He was born in Circleville, Ohio on September 24, 1914. He began singing on the radio in 1931, and favored a cowboy image.

In 1949, Lee, came to radio station WWVA Wheeling and the World's Original Jamboree. Lee remained with the program for 25 years. From 1953 to 1969, Moore also served as WWVA's all night deejay where he gained his nickname, "The Coffee Drinking Night Hawk", sometimes tossing in a solo vocal performance accompanied by his own guitar or resonator guitar. Lee recorded extensively from 1953. Much of his output appeared on smaller labels with limited distribution. Lee's first record, "The Cat Came Back," was recorded in 1953. The song was recorded out of necessity: he had been playing a record of it by Yodeling Slim Clark on his radio program. Because it was requested so often, he wore out his only copy and was unable to find an-other – so he recorded the song himself.

Lee spent the last 23 years of his life near Troy, New York and passed away August 17, 1997.

**Circa late 1950's "Lee Moore" guitar, dark natural finish with black scene, unusual trapeze tailpiece. Wording on body reads: "Lee Moore, 'The Lonesome Cowboy,'. Distributed by Tomchin Furniture Co., Princeton, West Virginia.**

# "LARIAT" GUITAR
## as Sold by
## Montgomery Ward

From the spring of 1957 through the fall of 1958, Wards offered the "Lariat" model guitar. The Lariat was made by Harmony for Wards. Its scene showed cowboys on horseback roping cattle. In the background were big cacti and a big sunrise. Above the scene the word "Lariat" was painted in rope letters. The scene was painted in cream and tan on the brown sunburst birch body. White striping was painted around the top edge and soundhole. Sometimes the peghead had a Gibsonesque "fleur-de-lis" painted in white. Three Harmony-style position makers were painted on the rosewood colored fretboard. The chrome plated trapeze tailpiece with heart cutouts is another Harmony identifier.

The guitar was standard size (35 3/4" X 13 1/4") and was advertised as a beginner's guitar. The fall 1957 Wards catalog stated, "You'll get a thrill out of playing calypso music, Rock 'N Roll or ballads on an easy-to-play low-priced guitar that has good tone".

**Spring of 1957 "Lariat" guitar, light brown sunburst with scene painted in tan and cream, standard size, 35 3/4" long, Harmony tailpiece and position markers, note Gibsonesque "fleur-de-lis" painted on peghead, sold through Wards.**

# "WESTERN REX"

This same scene had also been used on a "Western Rex" 3/4 size (32" X 11 1/2") guitar, but it did not show the Lariat name. This guitar was made by the Harmony Company and was available through an outlet other than Wards. The body was made of birch and was finished in a brown sunburst. The three-color scene was painted in cream, red and green. A white stripe was painted on the top edge of the body and around the soundhole. The neck had a peghead with the name "Western Rex" painted in cream color. The ebonized fretboard had four inlaid pearloid position dots. The rosewood colored wooden pin bridge was the stationary type, with a piece of fret wire for a saddle.

**Rex Allen, The Arizona Cowboy**

**Circa 1950 "Western Rex", small size guitar, 32" long, sunburst finish with scene in cream, red and green, pin bridge, made by Harmony.**

**1950's "Lariat" style scene, no name shown on body or peghead, standard size, 35 3/4" long, sunburst with scene in cream, red and green, triangular position markers like on Ward's "Lone Ranger" model, made by Harmony.**

# "ROUND UP"

The same scene had also been used on a guitar advertised in the circa 1939 Harmony catalog, the name "Round-up" was painted on the scene instead of "Lariat". The Harmony "Round-up" was a standard size birch guitar finished in opalescent gray with the two-color scene stenciled on top. The name Harmony was painted in white on the peghead. The fretboard had a crystalline finish with stenciled position markers. The strings attached to a nickel-plated "Idento" tailpiece and crossed over a moveable wooden bridge.

**Fall of 1939 "Round-up", "Pastime" name painted on peghead, "Round-up" name painted on body, same scene as used on Harmony's "Lariat", floral position markers painted on fretboard, made by Harmony.**

**Spring of 1948 "Lariat", all black guitar with scene painted in brown, white and green, no name painted on peghead, "Idento" tailpiece, made by Harmony.**

# "STAMPEDE" MODEL GUITAR
## as Sold by
## T. Eaton Company

From the fall of 1955 through the spring of 1962, Eaton offered a "Stampede" guitar. The "Stampede" was made by the Harmony Company of Chicago, Illinois, and had the same scene as Harmony's "Lariat" and "Western Rex" models, except for the name "Stampede" painted at the lower right of the scene. The "Stampede" was a very large, grand concert (39 1/8" X 15 1/4") size guitar and had fourteen frets clear of the body. The birch guitar had a sunburst finish with the scene painted in cream and red. A cream-colored stripe was painted on the top edge of the body with a double stripe painted around the soundhole. The pinless stationary bridge was ebonized as was the fretboard. Snowflake position markers were painted on the fretboard and a Gibsonesque "fleur-de-lis" was painted on the peghead.

**1958 "Stampede" big grand concert size guitar (39 1/4" X 15"), "Stampede" name painted on body, note Gibonesque "fleur-de-lis" painted on peghead and "Snowflake" position markers painted on fretboard, made by Harmony.**

**Circa fall of 1955 through spring of 1962 "Stampede", brown sunburst birch guitar with scene painted in cream and red, pinless bridge as used on Harmony's "Roy Rogers" guitar, made by Harmony.**

# "KING OF THE WEST" GUITAR
## as Sold by
## T. Eaton Company (Made in Canada)

From the fall of 1959 through the spring of 1961, Eaton offered the "King of the West" guitar. The standard size (36 1/2" X 13 1/4") guitar was made of birch and stained a light walnut color. The scene was painted in black and red and showed a royal Canadian Mountie atop a reared-up horse. Mountains and trees were visible in the background and the words "King of the West" were painted in the upper right. The guitar had a metal trapeze tailpiece (this particular style of tailpiece is one way to identify the guitar as being made in Canada) with a moveable wooden bridge. The ebonized fretboard has three silver position dots painted on.

The "King of the West" guitar came as an outfit, which included a Hawaiian steel bar and an extension nut, three finger picks and one flat pick, and extra set of strings, two instruction books, six assorted music-and-words folios, and multicolored neck cord – all for $17.95 Canadian dollars, delivery included.

This guitar was sold in outlets other than Eaton as early as 1957.

1957 "King of the West" guitar, standard size, 36 1/2" long, three position dots painted in silver on ebonized fretboard, shiny metal trapeze tailpiece, birch body, made in Canada.

1957 "King of the West" model, light walnut stained sunburst with a black and red scene showing a Royal Canadian Mountie.

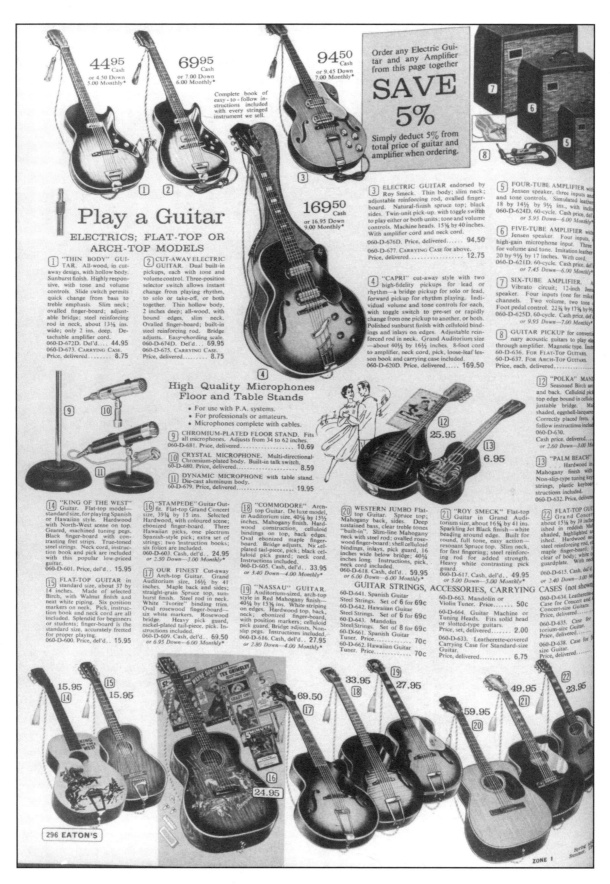

T. Eaton's 1961 spring and summer catalog shows a "King of the West"
Canadian-made cowboy guitar and a "Stampede" U.S.-made cowboy guitar.

# "LARIAT" GUITAR

## as Sold by

## T. Eaton Company (Made in Canada)

For the fall of 1961, Eaton offered a "Lariat" model guitar. The standard size (36 1/2" X 13 1/4") birch guitar had a sunburst finish with a cream colored scene and white striping painted around the top edge and soundhole. The scene showed a cowboy on horseback waving his hat above his head while lassoing a horse. The lasso makes a huge oval shape, which intersects the soundhole. The word "Lariat" was painted under the lower right-hand side of the soundhole and was given the appearance of being spelled out in rope. On the right of the scene was a cactus and a distant mountain range. The guitar had a shiny metal trapeze shaped tailpiece with a moveable wooden bridge. Three silver position dots were painted on the ebonized finger-board. The peghead had a very simple Gibson-like shape with three-on-a-side plank tuning keys with white plastic buttons.

Note: The "Lariat" guitar was sold through outlets other than Eaton as early as 1958. An early version had a natural finish top with scene painted in black.

Circa late 1950's "Lariat" model guitar, standard size 36 1/2" long, three silver colored position dots on ebonized fretboard, shiny metal trapeze tailpiece, made in Canada.

1958 oval date stamp
inside Canadian-made
"Lariat" model guitar.

1958 "Lariat" guitar, natural finish birch body
with scene painted in black, made in Canada.

# "TRAIL DRIVER" GUITAR

## as Sold by

## T. Eaton Company (Made in Canada)

From the spring of 1962 through the spring of 1963, Eaton's offered a "Trail Driver" model guitar. The standard size (36 1/2" X 13 1/8") birch guitar had a honey colored sunburst finish. The gold colored scene showed a team of mules pulling a covered wagon with a bearded wagon driver reminiscent of Gabby Hayes. A cactus and rough mountainous terrain helped frame the scene, with the words "Trail Driver" in the lower right-hand portion. White striping was painted around the top edge of the body and soundhole. Three silver position dots were painted on the ebonized fretboard. The guitar had a shiny metal trapeze shaped tailpiece with a moveable wooden bridge.

1962 "Trail Driver" standard size 36 1/2" long, body made of birch, three silver position dots painted on ebonized fretboard, shiny metal trapeze tailpiece, made in Canada.

1962 "Trail Driver", honey colored sunburst with gold colored scene and white striping, made in Canada, sold through T. Eaton.

# MASTRO "WESTERN GUITAR"
## as Sold by
## Spiegel

During Christmas of 1966 Spiegel offered the all-plastic "Western Guitar". This guitar was made by Mastro, a New York company owned and operated by the famous guitar maker Mario Maccaferri.

The guitar had an ivory colored top and peghead with a "rosewood" swirly brown colored back. The scenes were painted in red and blue. The guitar top had a combination of several scenes, including a cowboy falling off a horse, a pistol, an "M" branding iron, a cowboy playing guitar with a cowgirl singing, a covered wagon, a pair of cowboy boots, a cowboy hat, a saddle, and a rope design encircling the top edge. On the peghead was the name "Mastro", the model name "Western Guitar" and a small caricature of a guitar playing cowboy with an "M" as his body, also shown were the words "patented" and "Made in USA".

The "Western Guitar" was 31" in total length. The friction-type tuning pegs were white with an "M" (for Mastro) on each key. Spiegel offered the "Western Guitar" with multicolored neck cord, pick, instruction and song book, all for $3.97.

**Circa 1966 Mastro "Western Guitar",
all plastic guitar, produced by Mario Maccaferri's
company in New York, ivory colored top with
cowboy scenes in red and blue.**

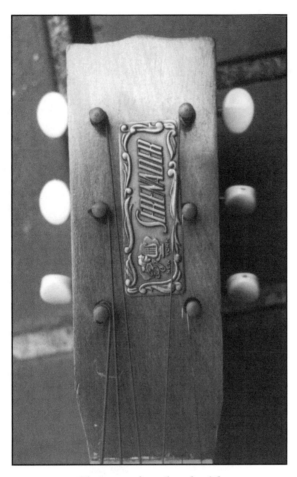

Closeup of peghead with
"Serenader" brass name plate.

Circa 1957 Serenader cowboy guitar
made by United, label inside
shows it was sold through
Fritz J. Hauck of Cincinatti.

Closeup of label inside
1957 Serenader reads
"Aida, Mandolins and
Guitars, Fritz J. Hauck Sole
Agent, Cincinnati, Ohio".

Mid 1950's United Elitone, with cowboy on bucking bronco scene, walnut stained birch guitar with dark brown scene and white striping, typical United trapeze tailpiece.

Close-up of peghead of mid 1950's "United" cowboy guitar.

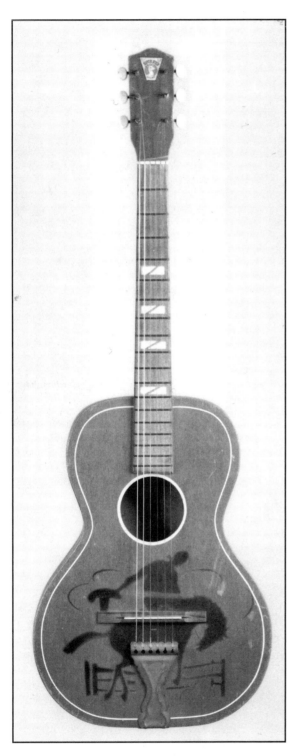

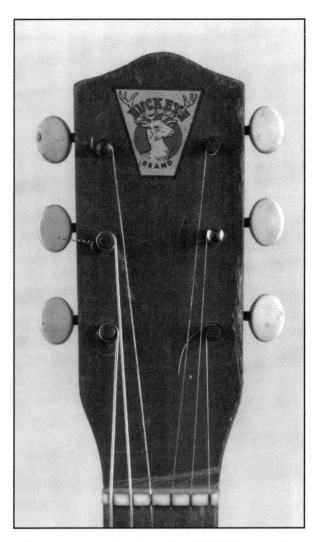

Close-up of peghead of circa 1957 "Buckeye" distributed by Grossman Music of Cleveland, made by United.

Circa 1957 cowboy guitar, 36 3/4" long, this scene can be found on guitars with brand names of Buckeye, United, Royalist, Stadium and a few others – all made by United.

Close-up of cowboy on horseback caricature on peghead of circa 1950's "Laredo" guitar.

Circa 1950's "Laredo" guitar, all black with white accents, made by United.

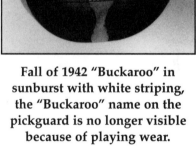

Fall of 1942 "Buckaroo" in sunburst with white striping, the "Buckaroo" name on the pickguard is no longer visible because of playing wear.

Circa 1950's "Laredo" guitar in sunburst finish, cowboy caricature on peghead and triangular position markers painted on fretboard, 36 3/4" total length, made by United.

Circa 1940's "buckaroo" archtop guitar, natural finish with black striping, 40 1/4" long, the name "Buckaroo" is painted in red on the pickguard and with a cowboy stencil on the peghead, white block markers painted on fretboard, made by Harmony.

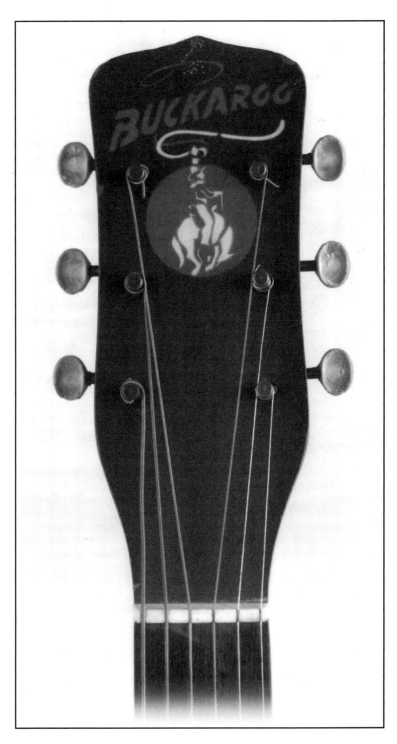

Circa 1940's "Buckaroo" caricature is similar to that of a 1930's Gene Autry peghead, open-back Kluson keys with white buttons ready to crumble.

Peghead of circa 1940's "two Indians" model shows the "Serenader" name. Kluson key buttons are about to crumble with age.

Circa 1940's Serenader "two Indians" model, very art deco, made by Harmony and distributed by Bugeleisen & Jacobson of New York. Art work shows two Indians with headdresses and bows, upper portion of guitar body is painted black and lower portion is walnut color with painted flame effect.

Circa 1940's "two Indians" label reads: "THE SERENADER, B. & J., NEW YORK" and shows a girl on a balcony serenaded by a young man.

February 1940 "Corral/Rodeo Scene" guitar, bronze color with cream colored scene, made by Richter.

1936 Vaquero "Amateur Hour", sunburst finish with white scene and striping, note lightning bolt soundholes.

1937 Vaquero "Spanish Model" shows a guitar player serenading a Spanish dancer on the lower bouts, and a sombrero on each of the upper bouts. Scene is painted in white on a brown sunburst finish, made by Kay, sold through Spiegel.

Circa late 1930s "Boots and Saddle" guitar. Printed in red is an inscription which reads "BOOTS AND SADDLE". Guitar is dark gray with scene in white and red. Guitar measures 37" x 14 1/4". Note unusual position markers.

"Ranger" cowboy guitar,
brown sunburst with scene
stenciled in white, trapeze
tailpiece, slot peghead.

Canadian-made cowboy guitar, natural finish birch
top with black cowboy scene, slotted peghead..

Circa 1969 German-made
cowboy guitar, natural finish
with scene in black,
distributed by Voss in
Dortmund, Germany.

Early 1940's beautiful "Corral Scene" guitar, this one is red with cream and black scene and white striping, pin bridge with wooden bridge pins, solid peghead with no label, made by Regal.

Circa 1942 Regal "Corral Scene" guitar, army green with cream and black scene and white striping, slotted peghead with dark green and gold Regal label, three green tree position markers painted on the ebonized fretboard.

Circa 1940's "Mariachi Guitar Player" scene, standard size 37" long, three inlaid position dots, slotted peghead, made in Canada.

Circa 1940's Canadian-made guitar, natural finished birch top with "Mariachi" scene painted in black and gold, walnut color stained back and sides.

# RED BELCHER

## Made by Regal

Finley "Red" Belcher was a well-known singer/banjo player in Kentucky. In 1937 he was doing hillbilly music on radio station WDZ in Tuscola, IL. He went on to perform on radio stations KWTO in Springfield, MO, WJJD in Chicago, IL, WWVA in Wheeling, WV, and WSVA in Harrisonburg, VA. One of Red's early groups was called the Kentucky Coon Skinners and his most popular group was called the Kentucky Ridgerunners. Red Belcher died in an automobile accident in 1952.

Circa early 1940's "Red Belcher" guitar, made by Regal. The silk screened artwork shows a quaint cottage with rising chimney smoke, hills, trees and a few distant birds. At the bottom of the scene is the name "Red Belcher's Favorite" spelled out in vine cuttings. The front of the guitar is a cream color with art in green and a slight red tint in the sky. The back of the guitar is an olive green color. The pin bridge and the fretboard are ebonized and the peghead is slotted.

Close-up of circa 1950's Rancher peghead, plank style tuners attached with nails helps identify it as being made by United.

Circa 1950's Rancher "Pal O'Mine" uke, natural finish top with brown scene and white striping, peghead detail in white, gold and red. Made of birch, 22 3/4" long, made by United.

Circa 1950's Rancher, 36 1/2" long birch guitar. Natural finish with brown scene and white striping, tailpiece helps to identify it as being made by United.

**Fall of 1957 "Black Stallion", black with scene painted in white, 35 3/4" long, pinless bridge, painted on triple-bar-sandwich position markers, made by Harmony, sold through Alden's catalog sales.**

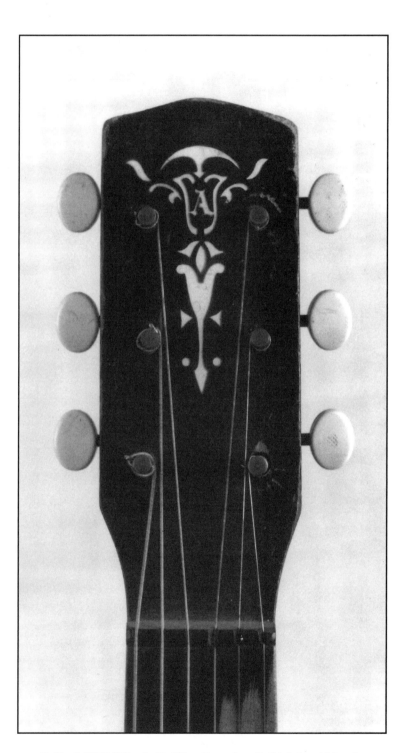

**Fall of 1957 "Black Stallion" peghead, "A" for Alden's.**

"Howdy Doody" ukes, made by Emenee, 17" long, one is off-white with an orange back and the other is green with an orange back, the scene is red, black and white and shows Howdy Doody playing guitar and Clarabell playing maracas, note original cardboard box with leather appearance.

Early 1950's "On The Range" cowboy ukulele, green fiberboard body with scene in yellow and brown, 19" in length, early model put out by Jefferson Manufacturing of Philadelphia, PA.

Closeup of late 50's "Zorro" peghead, made by Emenee.

Late 1950's "Zorro" guitar made by Emenee, four string plastic guitar.

Circa 1950's "Texan" brown sunburst with white scene and striping, 37" long, note unusual placement of the four position markers, made in Holland.

Pair of early 1950's Jefferson guitars. "Texan Jr." 30 1/2" long and the "Texan" a very large guitar for the Jefferson Company at 35" long.

Four year old Michael Evans is shown here with a 1956 "Texan Jr." guitar. Jefferson Manufacturing made at least three different versions of the "Texan Jr.". This model's scene shows a young cowboy and cowgirl and was available during the late 1950's. The 31" long fiberboard guitar had an orange to cream sunburst finish with a green scene and yellow rope design.

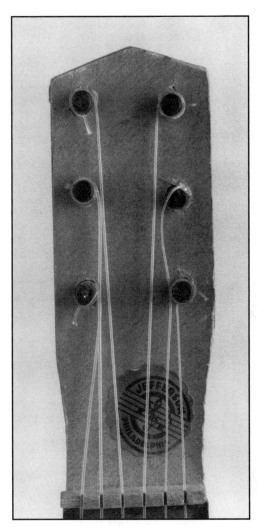

1950's old style Jefferson peghead with round "Jefferson" label.

Storytelling cowboys in Texas, 1910.

Pair of "Wyatt Earp" guitars, four and six string models, made by Jefferson Manufacturing, circa '59-'68.

Circa 1959 through 1968 "Wyatt Earp" fiberboard guitar, 30" long black to cream sunburst with red scene and yellow rope design and yellow position dots, made by Jefferson Manufacturing.

Young Jimmie (left) and Stevie Ray Vaughan in a family photo. Stevie Ray practices his licks on a Jefferson "Wyatt Earp" guitar.

Late 50's or early 60's Jefferson fiberboard banjo, 23 1/2" long, green to cream sunburst with red scene and yellow rope design, green tailpiece.

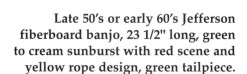

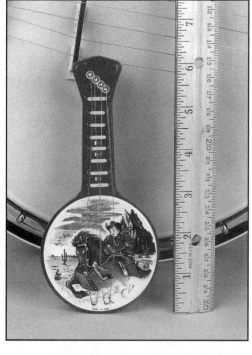

Miniature tin banjo with a multicolored lithographed scene, showing a young cowboy riding his horse at top speed, made in Japan.

Late 50's or early 60's fiberboard banjo, brown to cream sunburst with green scene and yellow rope design, brown tailpiece, made by Jefferson Manufacturing.

Gregg Hopkins receiving his first guitar, a Wyatt Earp model, on December 25, 1958.

1950's fiberboard cowboy "bull fiddle", 36 1/4" long, orange to cream sunburst with green scene and yellow rope design, made by Jefferson.

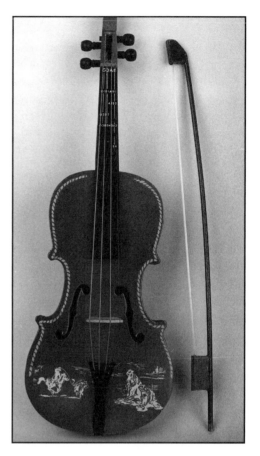

Late 50's or early 60's "cowboy violin" made by Jefferson, 22" in total length, orange colored fiddle with cowboy scene in green, and a rope design in yellow around top edge.

Mattel "Strum-Fun Getar" with original box, copyright 1959, 20" long, came with eight different song discs.

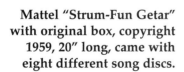

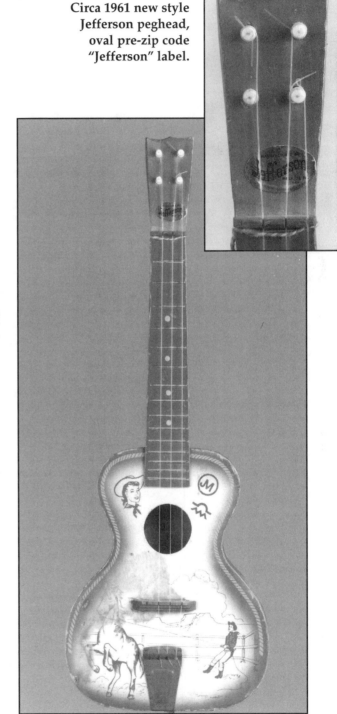

Circa 1961 new style Jefferson peghead, oval pre-zip code "Jefferson" label.

Circa 1957 fiberboard guitar with an intricately detailed wagon train scene, a moose and an eagle are also shown. The scene is done in brown on this bright yellow guitar. Peghead label reads "A Range Rhythm Toy, Tupelo, Miss, U.S.A.," although the factory's official name was "Rich Toy Company" of Tupelo. The original box is ink-stamped giving information as to this guitar being model #22W.

Circa 1961 cowboy guitar, "Circle JM" brand for Jefferson Manufacturing, orangish brown sunburst with green scene and yellow rope design, 24 7/8" long. Was also available in green sunburst.

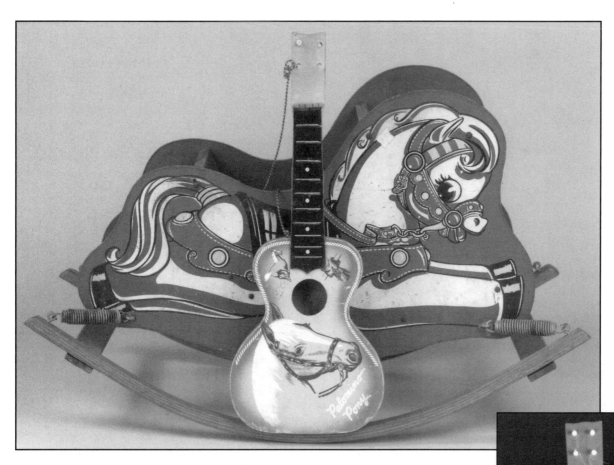

Late 1960's "Palomino Pony" orange to cream sunburst, 22 1/8" long, slightly smaller than the early 60's model which was available in four or six strings, made by Jefferson Manufacturing and is still being produced today.

1996 "Texan Jr." made by Jefferson, 28 1/2" long, orange to cream sunburst with brown and white scene, note fancy "wagon wheel and floral" (post 1983) position markers, this scene was introduced in 1966.

1960's "Bronco Bill" guitar, orange to cream sunburst with green scene and yellow rope design, black tailpiece, made by

Pint-size cowboy guitar, 7 3/4" in length, plastic with raised cactus motifs, reddish brown swirl top, teal green back.

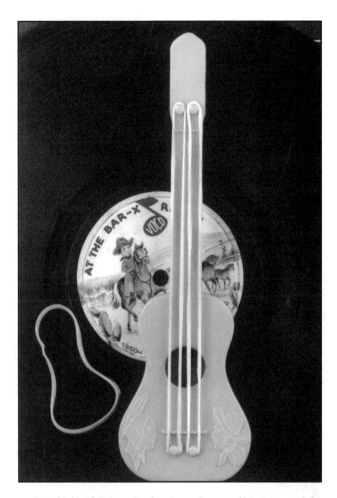

Small (7 3/4" long) plastic guitar, yellow top with a blue back, raised images of an Indian on left side and a cowboy on the right side, this type of guitar was referred to as a rubber band guitar, because rubber bands were used as strings.

Even "Woody" likes to strum a tune on his cowboy guitar.

Cowboy banjo, 15" long, body made of tin, fiberboard fingerboard attached to wooden neck.

1997 "Roundup Time" banjo by Jefferson, 23 1/2" long, brown to cream sunburst with cowboy scene in brown, round soundhole on back of fiberboard body, slotted peghead with friction tuning pegs.

Metal cowboy guitar measures 14 1/4" long, made of tin; colors are orange, cream, brown and yellow; red fiberboard fretboard attached to wooden neck.

Marc Bristol – Feel Like Flying

Marc Bristol, from hat to boots…all cowboy!

Metal cowboy guitar, like the model to the left, but this one has a different scene and a tin fretboard.

Late 1960's Jefferson "Rodeo" uke, bright yellow with art done in red (was also available in red with white art or blue with yellow art), scene shows rodeo action with two cowboys on bucking broncos, grandstands visible in background, 17" long, typical Jefferson construction with fiberboard body and wooden neck.

An Indian Chief is shown on this toy uke, also shown is a speeding stagecoach (as if being chased by Indians) and colorful designs. 14 1/2" long, body and fretboard made of tin, neck is wooden, instrument is red with art work in several colors, made in Japan.

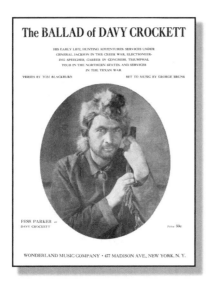

# Davy Crockett
# King of the Wild Frontier!

*"...Raised in the woods so's he knew ev'ry tree,*
*kilt him a b'ar when he was only three..."*
*"...He give his word an' he give his hand*
*that his injun friends could keep their land..."*
*"...He went off to Congress an' served a spell*
*fixin' up the Gover'ment an' laws as well..."*
*"...Where freedome was fightin' another foe*
*an' they needed him at the Alamo..."*

©1954 Walt Disney Productions

Circa 1956 "Davy Crockett" guitar, Range Rhythm made by Rich Toy Company, bright yellow fiberboard with wood fretboard and neck.

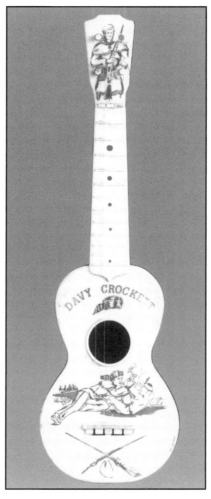

Circa mid 1950's "Davy Crockett" uke, 17" long, cream colored plastic with red and brown scene, back is dark swirly brown.

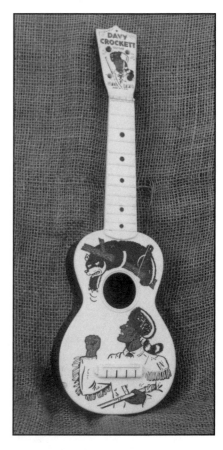

"Davy Crockett" plastic guitar, caricature of Davy Crockett on peghead, main scene shows Davy with coon skin cap and rifle, looking up at bear perched on tree limb, cream colored top with art work in brown, back of instrument is brown marbleized color, 15" in

Circa 1955 "Davy Crockett" with original box, wooden bell-shaped body, Davy Crockett "patched up the crack in the Liberty Bell," according to the song, "The Ballad of Davy Crockett."

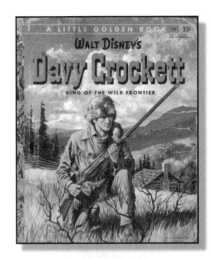

**1955 Book**

"Davy Crockett" crank uke, brown with multi-colored applique.

Mattel "Davy Crockett" plastic ukes: an all black one and a more rare yellow w/black back model. Both have the same brown multicolored applique showing Fess Parker as Davy Crockett from the 1950's Walt Disney TV programs and movies. Crank plays "Davy Crockett, King of the Wild Frontier."

Hank Williams Sr. and Hank Jr.
Hank Sr. has the Marin and Hank Jr. has
the copper plastic crank "ge-tar."

These two plastic crank cowboy "ge-tars" were made by Mattel from 1948 through 1953. They were available with different music box songs – usually "Bury Me Not On The Lone Prairie" or "Red River Valley". They measure 14" in length. On the left is circa 1948 through 1951 and is copper in color, the all black one on the right can be identified as circa 1952 through 1953, because it does not have the six shooters and steer's head above the soundhole.

Late 1950's or early 1960's "Rodeo" plastic guitar with an original carton, made by Emenee, scene in red, blue and black on a white top, the back is black with white swirls and the neck is black.

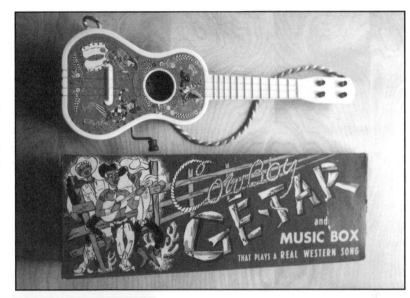

Mid 1950's Mattel "cowboy ge-tar" with original box, white with gold foil applique, crank plays "On Top Of Old Smokey".

Circa 1952 through 1953 copper-colored Mattel crank "ge-tar" plays "Oh! Susanna", attached yellow and red neck cord.

This "cowboy ge-tar" was made by Mattel from 1953 through 1954. It was available in three different colors; "desert white, buckskin yellow, and sunburst red" and was also available with different crank songs. This one is white with a black applique, shown here with it's original box.

Disney cowboy guitar as sold in Japan, 18 1/2" long, with scene showing Mickey Mouse and Donald Duck as singing cowboys. Huey, Luey, Duey and three Dalmation puppies are dancing to music. Original box has great graphics also.

Early 1980's Mickey Mouse "Hi Kickin' Toy Banjo", 21" long, yellow with black back, applique shows Mickey and Minnie dancing, Goofy playing banjo and Donald on fiddle, all four characters are shown in western attire.

"Mickey Mousegetar," 29 3/4" long, black plastic with brown and multi-colored applique, shows Mickey dressed in cowboy attire happily strumming a guitar, authorized by Walt Disney, made by Carnival. Note the little "Cowboy Mickey" wind up plastic figure with original box. He strums his guitar when wound.

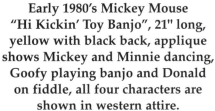

This "Little West" guitar and harmonica set was put out by Ohio Art in 1983. The guitar has a horse head shaped body and a horseshoe-shaped peghead. When held in the playing position, a dial is located where the right hand would strum (if it were a real guitar). Turning the dial operates an internal music box which plays "Home on the Range." The accompanying harmonica is ingeniously shaped like a moustache, to add an interesting visual effect when played.

"Lil' Cowboy" Copyright 1988 plastic toy guitar, made by Superior Toy Company, 15 1/2" long.

Peghead of late '50s "Wrangler" with an upside down Range Rhythm label, made by Rich Toy Company's factory in Chicago, IL.

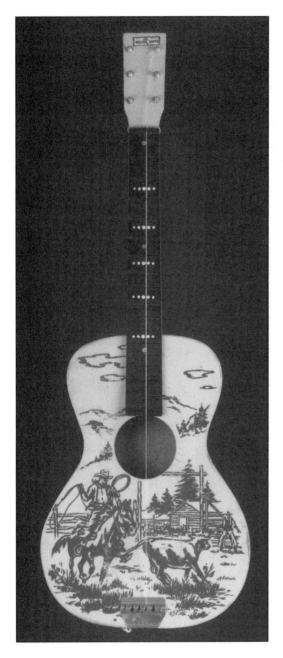

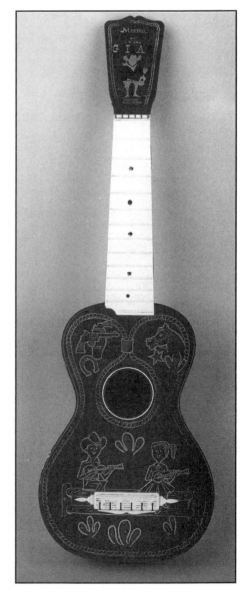

Late '50s Range Rhythm "Wrangler", 30 1/2" long, fiberboard guitar, bright yellow with brown scene.

Mid 1960's Mastro cowboy guitar, red with cream colored bridge and fingerboard, 21" long, western scenes done in white and green, show a cowboy and girl playing guitars while sitting on a fence, a pair of pistols with holster, a horse shoe, horse, and several cacti. The wording on the peghead reads "Mastro Jr. Guitar, designed by Maccaferri" and shows a caricature of a cowboy (an "M" for his body) with one hand holding a guitar and the other hand ready to draw his pistol.

Guitar made of tin, lithographed with an attractive scene, shows a US calvary soldier with rifle in arms and riding a horse, a stage coach, an Indian with bow & arrow riding horse, a flowering cactus plant, and an Indian with spear riding a horse, 17 3/4" long, made in Japan.

Plastic cowboy guitar with the name "Folk Guitar" on peghead, 29" long, beige and black guitar with cowboy scene in tan and brown, note cowboy drum in background.

Carnival plastic cowboy uke, 15 1/2" long, red swirl front with black back. Its decal shows some cowboys sitting around a campfire singing and one playing banjo.

Cowgirls just want to have fun!

"Cowboy Ge-Tar", bright blue with multi-colored scene, showing a young cowboy on horseback. Original 1972 box was designed with an opening so a potential purchaser could turn the crank and hear a tune (Red River Valley).

1966 Mattel cowboy uke, black plastic with yellow applique showing eleven young cowboys, crank plays "On Top Of Old Smokey".

Pair of plastic crank guitars with raised cowboy
motifs, yellow with red motif on left, brown
with black motif on right. Made by Knickerbocker
Plastic Company of Glendale, California.

Fall of 1950 plastic cowboy uke, red
front and yellow back, scene shows a
cowboy on a bucking bronc and a
cactus, 14 1/2" long, made by Reliable
Plastics Company in Canada, sold
through Eaton.

Carnival plastic uke with
original box, still has the
shrink wrap on.

191

Circa 1953. Carnival cowboy banjo, cream color with cowboy appliques, with original box.

Carnival plastic banjo with cowboy applique, red swirl colored top and blue swirl colored back, black tuning pegs, shown here with original box.

Circa 1960's "Hootenanny" plastic uke with a very cute country music scene, 17" long, made by Carnival.

Circa 1953. Carnival brand uke with cowboy appliques, cream colored plastic.

Saguaro cacti! 15 1/2" plastic banjo with yellow front and green back, decal shows three cowboys around the camp fire. Raised cacti images set off the little 7 1/2" bright green and yellow guitar. Interesting western lamp in background is shaped like a wagon.

Circa 1973 Carnival cowboy uke with red and black cowboy decorations on top, 15 1/4" long, all plastic, ivory colored top with black back, in the early '80s this same uke was available in a bright yellow.

Circa 1973 Carnival brand plastic uke, 15 1/4" long, cream colored with dark gray back, peghead scene in blue and red shows a young cowboy playing a uke, this model was called the "Li'l Cowboy" uke. It also came in bright yellow in the early '80s.

"Singing Cowboy" plastic guitarette, small decal shows a cowboy about to get thrown from his horse, the 14" plastic toy guitar has a light blue front with a yellow back, this original box has some great graphics.

Circa 1956 Carnival brand "Home on the Range" plastic uke, 15 1/2" long, uke has a cream front with a brown back, cowboy scenes are in red and brown.

Circa 1982 "Willie Nelson" plastic guitar, multi-colored applique, white top with black neck and back, 29 1/2" long, friction tuning pegs, there was also a deluxe "Willie Nelson" with geared tuners, made by Carnival.

TRIVIA: Willie Nelson calls his well played Martin guitar (Model N-20) "Trigger".

Early 1980's "Do-si-do" banjo made by Carnival.
15 1/2" plastic banjo, bright yellow and black
with scene in red and blue.

Circa 1973 "Swing Your Partner," red, white
and blue plastic banjo, 22 1/2" long.

A couple of interesting plastic cowboy guitars, still in original packaging.

# JEFFERSON MANUFACTURING
## New Issue Guitars

"Gene Autry" limited edition guitar, made by Jefferson Manufacturing, brand new for 2000, this one made in March of 2000 and has a limited edition number of 161. Silk screened photo of Gene playing guitar is printed in black, white and red. Red was used, because it was Gene's favorite color. The words "America's Favorite Singing Cowboy, 1907-1998", the name "Gene Autry" outlined by a red star, and a large red letter "A" with attached wings, are printed on the guitar. "Flying A's" are also used as position markers on the fretboard. The guitar is 28" in total length. This is the first Jefferson "theme" guitar to have a wooden (gum laminate) top, instead of fiberboard,

"Hopalong Cassidy" guitar, "authorized issue" made by Jefferson, brand new for 2000, this one made in March of 2000 and has limited edition number of 104. It has a great black & white photo of Bill Boyd as Hopalong Cassidy shown with his horse, Topper. The art work is silk screened on the black & cream sunburst guitar. Wording printed in white reads "Hoppy 1895-1972" and "The – 20 Ranch". Wording in black and encircling the sound hole reads "Hopalong Cassidy & Topper". Guitar is 28" long, has five "steer's head" fretboard markers adorning the neck, a small gold-foil label on the peghead reads "Over 50 Years, Manufactured by Jefferson, Phila.,

"Roy Rogers" reissue guitar by Jefferson, introduced in 1999, this one was made in March of 2000. It has several differences from the late 1960's model: "RR" fretboard markers, slotted peghead with tuning keys on sides, and inscription reading "King Of The Cowboys, 1911-1998" located where Dale's face had been on the old model. 28" in total length, limited edition label inside guitar, this one is number 2,766, is in a black (new for 2000) colored box.

# JEFFERSON MANUFACTURING
## New Issue Guitars

"Willie Nelson" guitar, new for 2001. This one was made in May of 2001. The art work includes Willie Nelson's face, his name, and a collage of Willie's hit song titles. Reading over them helps one realize how successful Willie's music career has been. The fretboard has the initials "WN" as position markers, The Willie Nelson guitar has a model number of W-74.'

"Lone Ranger" reissue, new for 2001. The guitar shown here has a limited edition number of #00304, made in May of 2001. Orange sunburst with black and white art work, almost identical in color to the original. Differentiating the new from the old. The 2001 model has the wording "Hi-yo Silver Away!", a white hat, black mask and silver bullet. Fretboard is 2" shorter and "Lone Ranger masks" position markers. Label reads "L-73, Lone Ranger, Limited Edition" and shows its number of sequence. The reissues are not identical to the originals, to discourage them from being resold on the secondary market

"Riders in the Sky" guitar, new for 2001. This one was made in May of 2001. Art work shows Woody Paul, Ranger Doug, Too Slim, and Joey the Cowpolka King. The guitar has a similar look to the "Roy Rogers" guitar with its orange sunburst and brown and white artwork all outlined by a white rope design. The guitar is 28" in total length and has a fiberboard body, wooden neck and a fretboard made of fiberboard. The fretboard has five "steer's head" position markers. The model number is S-76.

# JEFFERSON MANUFACTURING

Jefferson Manufacturing Company, 2433 North Orianna Street, registered its business in Philadelphia, Pennsylvania on February 21, 1945. Jefferson started out making toys, and in the early 1950's began concentrating on producing toy ukes and guitars. Robert Jefferson, the company founder, pioneered silk-screening methods which he used in the production of several different "theme" guitars. The majority of these were cowboy guitars, but Jefferson guitars were also produced with other interesting art. One model, called "The Twist," showed couples dancing to rock 'n roll music, while another model, called "Rocket Ranger," showed an outer space scene.

Due to ill health, Robert closed down the factory in 1981, but it reopened in 1983 with George Jefferson (son of Robert Jefferson) at the reins. Today, the business, still in its original building, continues the tradition with production of new cowboy guitars. At least nine different cowboy models and limited editions are currently available. George Jefferson has made an intriguing statement: "These guitars have been made the same way for the past 50 years, with virtually no change in the process."

**George Jefferson manning his booth at the "International Toy Fair" held February 2000 in New York City. George was introducing the new "Gene Autry" and "Hopalong Cassidy"**

**Barbara Jefferson, George's wife, assisting with the Jefferson Manufacturing booth at the International Toy Fair, February 2000.**

# HOPALONG CASSIDY

William Lawrence Boyd was born June 5, 1895 in Hendrysburg, Ohio. He moved to Oklahoma with his family at age 7. His father died when he was a teenager, in a mining accident at Tulsa. Bill, one of four children, dropped out of school to help support the family.

From age 12 on, he tried his hand at a variety of jobs around the country. In 1919 Boyd came to Hollywood. His first job was as an extra in a Gloria Swanson picture. His roles gradually improved and in 1926 he starred as a hero in *The Volga Boatman*. The picture was a hit.

It was another Bill Boyd who was arrested in 1932 for participation in a scandalous beach party – but the newspaper accounts confused William Boyd with his namesake and it seemed that the story, true or not, had washed up William Boyd's movie career as far as the public was concerned.

Harry 'Pop' Sherman acquired the rights to Clarence E. Mulford's 25 western books, one of which featured a sawed-off tobacco-spitting loudmouthed redhead with a straggly mustache and a gimpy leg called Hopalong Cassidy. Sherman offered the down-on-his-luck Boyd

the leading role in one of the features. Boyd, it was said, went after the part of Cassidy himself but laundered it from the book version into the easy-going experienced westerner. He must have been persuasive, because he wound up in the title role of Sherman's *Hop-A-Long Cassidy* film (Paramount, 1935).

Boyd wore a dark outfit along the lines of the early Tim McCoy, which contrasted with his white hair and white horse, Topper. His enduring old-timer sidekicks were Windy (George Hayes) and California Carlson (Andy Clyde).

In 1946 Boyd bought the rights to his Cassidy character and formed his own production company. Mortgaging his home and other property, Boyd bought television rights to his old films. Only Gene Autry had acted with similar foresight. Soon the Hoppy films were playing on 66 television stations, and he hit the trail with 52 30-minute Hoppy TV shows. He branched into radio, personal appearances, comic books, comic strips, and merchandising, retiring from show business in 1953. He sold his William Boyd Enterprises in 1958 for $8 million. On September 12, 1972, he died in a Laguna Beach, California hospital.

**Close up of neck detail with Ernie's signature at the last fret.**

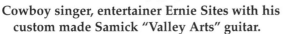

Cowboy singer, entertainer Ernie Sites with his custom made Samick "Valley Arts" guitar.

New issue from MBT International is this Stella, Harmony "Singing Cowboy Guitar". Made from select materials, this is an all black guitar with the art being one color, gray. Comes in an orange and black cardboard case. Made in China.

# COWBOY X, COWBOY II, AND COWBOY III

## C. F. Martin & Co.

The Cowboy X, Cowboy II, and Cowboy III guitars are Limited Edition models by Martin Guitar Company. These unique guitars feature a OOO-size body and take advantage of cutting edge HPL photo laminating technology to reproduce Robert Armstrong's vivid cowboy scenes. The back and sides are cut from a colored patterned HPL material to complement the color of the top. The neck is shaped from Stratabound®, a resin impregnated wood laminate with remarkable strength, and the fingerboard and bridge are crafted from specially formulated black Micarta®. The internal sound-board support utilizes solid spruce X-bracing with thin graphite plates to reinforce the bridge area. The tuning machines are black enclosed with black knobs. Each guitar has an interior label individually numbered in sequence with the edition total.

**Cowboy X, limited to 250 guitars. Martin's first cowboy edition depicts a traditional western campfire scene against a moonlit desert backdrop.**

**Cowboy II, limited to 500 guitars. The cook on the Cowboy II might look a bit familiar. It's C. F. (Chris) Martin IV feeding dinner scraps to a hungry trail dog, or perhaps it's a friendly coyote.**

**Cowboy III, limited to 750 guitars. Look closely at that bucking bronco and you'll see C. F. (Chris) Martin on top holding his own.**

Gibson
custom shop.

William S. Hart, Range
Rider of the Yellowstone,
early cowboy movie star
from 1917, illustrated on a
Gibson J-200.

Western sky guitar, hand carved top.

Frank and Jesse James

Butch Cassidy

Wyatt Earp

Gibson custom shop.

White Buffalo "Miracle"
Owner, Alan Levin, Fender custom shop.

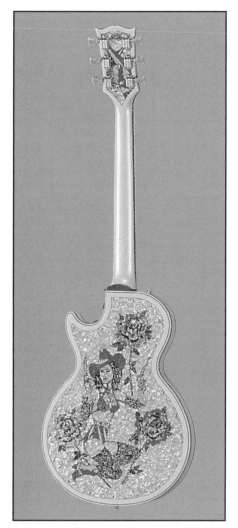

Gibson

Horseshoe Tele
Owner, Yamano Music, Japan
Fender

Pohaku Lone Ranger guitar
built by Peter Hurney

1971 Buck Owens "American" model with red,
white and blue finish, as seen on the "Hee Haw"
television show, 41" long, made by Harmony.
The original was made by Semie Moseley.

# GREG RICH

## Cowboy Guitar Designer

The national consciousness is indelibly stamped with the image of a small boy preparing to saddle up his trusty wooden rocking horse, swaggering in oversized cowboy boots and hat, Wranglers and pint-sized Western shirt while he gleefully bangs away on a cheap nylon-string guitar (dutifully painted with cacti or desert scenes). Inspiration for such youthful play-acting has been bound in countless Saturday matinee shoot-'em Westerns and singing celluloid cowboys like Gene Autry, Tex Ritter and Roy Rogers. But far from being the sole province of the under-10 set, cowboy guitars are also collector's items imbued with Hollywood's alluring mystique via those same improbably costumed stars. For a long time, their value lay in that link to Hollywood's myth of the West.

In recent years, however, cowboy guitars have evolved from mere novelty to coveted custom instruments for kids who've grown up to be mature, capable instrumentalists with a taste for history and a yen for style. At the forefront of that movement toward respectability is artisan Greg Rich. He's been earning accolades for his work with acoustic instruments since he was a teenager. The nationally re-nowned luthier's skill has transformed cowboy guitars from childhood prop to gallery-worthy art pieces.

Strange as it may seem, the much-lauded cowboy guitar designer spent his formative years in the tony seaside community of Newport Beach in Orange County, California. The area is rich with artists, including movie stars, and both the human and natural landscapes are blessed with vibrant color and a sense of unlimited possibility. Additionally, it's not far from working ranches where real cowboys still lasso cattle and go honky-tonkin'. Rich's affinity for the eye-popping 'rhinestone cowboy' aesthetic reflects that culture as well as the Hollywood world of country-and-western couturier Nudie Cohen.

Rich's launching pad into those flashy environs was the humble Boys Club, where he took a class in lapidary-the process of cutting, polishing or engraving gems. He was all of 12. By the time he was 14, his stone-cutting and design talents had generated enough buzz that a local jeweler hired him for a part-time job.

"By the time I was 14, I was submerging my wheels," Rich says, recalling a unique work technique he developed. "I'd put them under water and wear scuba goggles and cut black opal. I was cutting $50,000 pieces of opal. I had clients and a full-time gig by the time I was 15."

**Guitar Headstock featuring
a full Indian Headdress using wood,
pearl, and abalone.**

**Kahina Banjo back, hand carved and
painted, features the
Kahina Sun God**

207

**Handpainted guitar, called "Spirit Horse"**

**Leather cover tooled telestyle guitar designed by Greg Rich.**

Since "no one else was doing it," he began to study metal engraving and wood carving too, adding to his expanding list of instrument-enhancing skills. By 16, he was casting gold, metal and silver for a local company, and mastering the basics of inlay work. Clearly, "do it yourself" was more than a catch-phrase for him: it quite literally became a guiding principle for his career. Inspired by Larry McNeely's performance of "Arkansas Traveler" on a TV show, he picked up a banjo and started plunking away, finding his way around the neck as he practiced the warp-speed breakdowns of the day. He got turned on to Earl Scruggs and studied the differences in playing technique and their effect on sound. Learning to approach the instrument as a musician gave him deeper insights into its structure and the mechanics of its tonality, and soon people started bringing their banjos to him for repair. Once again, no one was available to give him formal instruction: so, while some of his peers were dismantling muscle cars with their dads and cobbling them back together, Rich taught himself how to build sturdy, resonant banjos. It wasn't long before people were bringing him their guitars as well, and consulting about binding, inlay, and fret details.

In 1987, after several years working in California and Texas, he was hired by Gibson Guitars to manage the banjo division of its custom shop in Nashville, Tennessee. It was an attention-getting event, since Rich was only 31 years old at the time. The famously conservative company entrusted him with complete responsibility for custom and artwork, repair and manufacturing details. From the beginning, he was a distinctive presence. His DIY ethic and let's-get-it-done approach also made him somewhat controversial, but he produced spectacular results. Drawing from his lengthy experience, he trained his hand-picked staff in everything from the intricacies of tone rings to scraping the skins to the proper selection and installation of tuners. During Rich's tenure, Gibson's sagging reputation was restored to its former prestige. Rich was able to produce high-end, elegantly crafted instruments to artists' demanding specs, and to place them directly in their hands. It was a valuable period that enhanced his national reputation as a custom-instrument luthier and gave him a name cachet. That followed him to Rich & Taylor and, ultimately, Dream Guitars.

Rich & Taylor was the company Rich formed with kindred spirit Mark Taylor (son of Tut Taylor) in 1993 when he left Gibson. Rich and Taylor immediately established a top-notch reputation. Sadly, as is all too often the case in instrument manufacturing, the economics of importing and shipping proved an insurmountable stumbling block, particularly given the increasing rarity of fine tone woods. However, the talented duo maintained their business connection: Taylor converted their company into Crafters of Tennessee. After a brief stint fashioning intricate designs for infamous guitar collector Mac Yasuda's company, Rich reemerged in 1998 with Dream Guitars, an acoustic instrument manufacturer whose specialty is custom art guitars. The Rich and Taylor team and ethic is still in place, as Crafters of Tennessee handles construction. As always, their goal is to build handcrafted instruments whose foremost attribute is superior quality of construction and tone, and they've achieved stunning results with the Recording King, a superb recreation of an old model banjo that has been used and praised by the likes of Herb Pedersen and Pat Cloud. Their acoustic guitars are likewise attracting attention. Rich is responsible for the guitars' design, and selecting and supervising the team of artisans who follow his blueprints. Rich handles the painstaking final stage of the guitars' creation–finishing, engraving, binding–that turns the instruments into unique art.

His work has been profiled in half a dozen national magazines and almost as many art books. The list of celebrities for whom he has designed or built guitars is quite literally star-studded: Gene Autry, Clint Black, Garth Brooks, James Burton, Little Jimmy Dickens, Holly Dunn, Stonewall Jackson, John Jorgenson, Paul McCartney, Sonny Osborne, Dolly Parton, Earl Scruggs, Frank Sinatra, Slash, Hank Snow, George Strait, Marty Stuart, Travis Tritt, Porter Wagoner, Hank Williams Jr. and Hank Williams III. Still others, Like Aerosmith's Steven Tyler, have been photographed with the limited-edition Rich & Taylor Roy Rogers guitar–perhaps the best-known of Rich's creations, as it has garnered the most press. The

**Opry star Porter Wagoner shows off his handmade guitar.**

**Greg Rich on stage at The Grand Ole Opry, presenting Porter his brand new Guitar. Mac Yasuda is in the center.**

**Billy Walker and his new guitar built by Rich and Taylor**

**Opry star Jimmy C. Newman and his handmade Cajun guitar.**

jumbo-style, hand-painted collectibles gleam with 24-karat gold-plated hardware, exotic inlays and excellent portraits of Roy Rogers, but the crowning touch is a label personally signed by the late Roy Rogers or Dale Evans. Just as important, the instruments don't sacrifice acoustic quality at the altar of artistic appeal. Considering their five-figure price tags, that little boy would get one hell of a whup-pin' if he tried bashing one of these on his rocking horse!

**Backstage at the Grand Ole Opry…
Jack Greene, Billy Walker,
Mac Yasuda, and Porter Wagoner
show off their new Art Guitars**

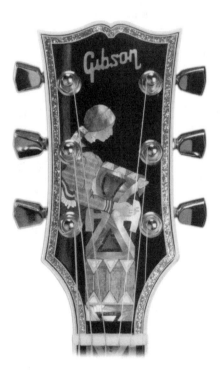

**Navajo Lady weaves a blanket,
inlaid into the headstock
of this Gibson Guitar.**

**Roy Rogers
guitar headstock.**

**Gene Autry headstock with
engraved silver and abalone.**

Greg Rich and Roy "Dusty" Rogers Jr. show
the brand new Roy Rogers Tribute Art Guitar.

Close up of the front
of the Roy Rogers guitar.

Close up of the back
of the Roy Rogers guitar.

Frank Stallone holds a brand new
Roy Rogers Art Guitar

Dale Evans and Greg Rich look over her new Tribute Guitar.

Greg Rich, Mac Yasuda, Gene Autry, Mrs. Gene Autry,
and Ed Gregory with the Gene Autry guitar

The Gene Autry guitar.

**Close up of the front of the Gene Autry guitar.**

**Close up of the back of the Gene Autry guitar.**

# THE COLLECTORS

We collect cowboy guitars for a variety of reasons. They might remind us of cowboy heroes we saw on TV as young children. Our first guitar most likely was one of the inexpensive guitars our folks bought for us at Christmas. Perhaps it was a birthday present that got lost on the road to growing up and we have to replace it, or we just like the art on the front. The reasons are as varied as the collector. In the guitar collecting world, these cowboy guitars are a real bargain and not likely to command very high prices. So it makes collecting guitars very affordable and it's fun as well.

Most of the following collectors collect other guitars. They may specialize in electrics, flat tops, arch tops, certain brands, certain dates, the list is as different as the individual. But these collectors all share one thing in common, whether they have just started their collection with their first guitar, have a couple, or a whole room full of them. There is no thrill as the discovery of a cowboy guitar. Here we highlight a small but dedicated following. They all enjoy the same guitars. We thank them all for sending in their photo of their prized possessions. In no particular order we present the cowboy guitar collectors.

**LeAnn Rimes relaxes and sings a song with her Long Ranger Guitar.**
**Photo by Ellen von Unwert**

Don Flick and his guitar collection.

Jesse Soest with his neat cowboy guitar collection.
Steve Soest photographer

Brian Fischer with a part of his large cowboy guitar collection.
Also his 1960 Caddy and Popeye the dog. Stephanie Fischer photographer

Tony Allan of Billinge, England may be the only collector of Cowboy Guitars in Great Britain. He is holding a pre-war (WWII) "The Plainsman." Center is a late 1940's Gene Autry "Melody Ranch." Far right is a Fall of 1932 "Gene Autry Round Up". This date, which is stamped inside, makes this particular model one of the earliest Cowboy Guitars to be made.

Ranger Doug, of Riders In The Sky, with his "Gene Autry" guitars. On the left is a circa 1955 plastic "Gene Autry-Cowboy Guitar" made by Emenee, and on the right is an early 50's Gene Autry "Melody Ranch"

Scott Waterhouse, Midwest Guitar Exchange. Photo: T.J. Mixon

Larry Briggs with a portion of his big cowboy guitar
collection. Larry owns and operates "Strings West" in
Tulsa, Oklahoma. Steve Evans photographer

Barry Haver of Bedford, Pennsylvania,
and his cowboy guitar collection.
Sally Haver photographer

Two singing cowboys from
camera shy Bud Johnson

A caption under this photo read
"World's Champion Woman-Hater, Albion L.
Clough, Ark of Maine at Cape Meddick."
No wonder his cowboy guitar
is the "Lone Ranger."

Leonard Coulson and his collection of
cowboy guitars on display at
"Intermountain Guitar
and Banjo" in Utah.
Kennard Machol photographer

Dale Cameron and son Jesse of Edmonton, Canada,
with their great cowboy guitar collection.
Patrick Vrouwe photographer

Eric and son, Evan, with the
Lenius cowboy guitar collection.
Eric, Diane and Evan Lenius have a
nice collection of cowboy guitars.
Matthew Sinn photographer

Chris Broadwell of Ithaca Guitar Works in Ithaca, New York, with several of his stencil-painted guitars.
Christopher Wright photographer

Gil Hembree and his cowboy guitar collection. Gil is holding a Gene Autry "Round Up" made in the fall of 1932. At top left is a 1930's "Lone Ranger," and at top right is a Harmony "Singing Cowboys."
Jane Hembree photographer

John Elling with his collection of cowboy guitars.
Jane Elling photographer

James Burkett of Alabama with his
cowboy guitar collection.
Eliot Burkett photographer

Eddie Montana from the "Liv'n It Up"
music store in Seal Beach, California.
John Lawrance photographer

John McGinty of North Little Rock, Arkansas
with his collection of cowboy guitars.
Steve Evans photographer

Frank Howell with his cowboy collection.

Don Skuce of Ed's Music Workshop.

John Nelson with his stencil guitars at a recent guitar show.

John Hargiss with his cowboy guitar collection. John owns Hargiss
Stringed Instruments in Omaha, Nebraska, and has a lot of cowboy
memorabilia displayed in his shop.
Paul Edwards photographer

Rob Friedman and his collection of cowboy guitars. Rob owns "Not
Just Another Music Shop" in Vancouver, British Columbia.
Randy Cole photographer

Professional musician Sylvain Acher
with his cowboy guitar collection.
Photographer Adam Henry
of Mark Alexander Photography

Singer Holly Dunn with her Roy Rogers
collectibles and guitar. Photo: Reserve Inc.

Doug Spencer of "I Buy Cowboy Guitars".
Steve Tillman photograper

Mike Stevens–master guitar builder, guitar collector, and cowboy–relaxes with his saddle and rare cowboy guitars. Mike was the first "recognized" cowboy collector. He displayed his collection at the Dallas, Texas Guitar Show in 1979.

Melissa Etheridge put it so well when she said, "Cowboy guitars bring art, music and nostalgia together." Melissa is shown here with her late 1930's "Plainsman" guitar.

Steve Evans with his favorite guitar to play. It is a one-of-a-kind Martin made in Martin's Custom Shop in 1995. The stenciled scene is appropriately entitled

Steve Evans being interviewd by Ayo Haynes for "Personal FX: The Collectibles Show". Steve was featured as a "Super Collector" with his collection of over 100 cowboy guitars. Kerri Margrave, photographer

# Test Your Horse Sense,

## correct answers

| Rider | Horse |
|---|---|
| William S. Hart | Fritz |
| Tom Mix | Tony |
| Ken Maynard | Tarzan the Wonder Horse |
| George O'Brien | Mike |
| Hoot Gibson | Mutt |
| Buck Jones | White Eagle |
| Fred Thompson | Silver King |
| Colonel Tim McCoy | Midnight |
| John Wayne | Duke |
| Tex Ritter | White Flash |
| Jack Hoxie | Scout |
| Buster Crabbe | Falcon |
| William "Hopalong Cassidy" Boyd | Topper |
| Clayton "The Lone Ranger" Moore | Silver |
| Rex Allen | Koko |
| Lash Larue | Rush, Back Diamond |
| Roy Rogers, "Smartest horse in the movies" | Trigger |
| Gene Autry, "Wonder horse of the West" | Champion |
| Dale Evans | Buttermilk |
| Duncan Renaldo "the Cisco Kid" | Diablo |
| Johnny Mack Brown | Rebel |
| Jimmy Wakely | Lucky |
| Eddie Dean | War Paint |
| Sunset Carson | Cactus |
| Joel McCrea "Texas Rangers" | Charcoal |
| Tim Holt | Lightning |
| Brisco County Jr. | Comet |
| Monte Hale | Partner |

**Jimmy Wakeley and Lucky**

**Rex Allen and Koko**

**The Cisco Kid and Diablo**

*When I lay down at night by a camp fire's light*
*And the work of the day is done*
*Then I wouldn't exchange my home on the range*
*For anything under the sun.*
*There's peace and rest out here in the west*
*Not found in your cities so grand*
*And when cowboys sing, the prairies ring*
*With music that I understand.*
—Carson J. Robison